THE ME OF TOMORROW

A Planning Manual for Your Future Life

Efrain Rovira *With* Nick Collins

THE ME OF TOMORROW
A PLANNING MANUAL FOR YOUR FUTURE LIFE

Copyright © 2021 Efrain Rovira With Nick Collins.

All rights reserved. No part of this book may be used or reproduced by any means, graphic, electronic, or mechanical, including photocopying, recording, taping or by any information storage retrieval system without the written permission of the author except in the case of brief quotations embodied in critical articles and reviews.

iUniverse books may be ordered through booksellers or by contacting:

iUniverse
1663 Liberty Drive
Bloomington, IN 47403
www.iuniverse.com
844-349-9409

Because of the dynamic nature of the Internet, any web addresses or links contained in this book may have changed since publication and may no longer be valid. The views expressed in this work are solely those of the author and do not necessarily reflect the views of the publisher, and the publisher hereby disclaims any responsibility for them.

Any people depicted in stock imagery provided by Getty Images are models, and such images are being used for illustrative purposes only.
Certain stock imagery © Getty Images.

ISBN: 978-1-6632-2904-5 (sc)
ISBN: 978-1-6632-2906-9 (hc)
ISBN: 978-1-6632-2905-2 (e)

Library of Congress Control Number: 2021919342

Print information available on the last page.

iUniverse rev. date: 03/11/2022

To my wife, kids, and parents. They have been my best teachers and the energy that fuels my life. Also to the many friends and family from whom I have learned how to live a better life.

I am grateful to my parents for teaching me the value of hard and honest work and why integrity matters. I am thankful to my mom for showing me the importance of caring about others. I am indebted to my dad for showing me never to stop dreaming. My wife is my best friend and the person who has always challenged me to be a better person, and I wouldn't be who I am without her.

CONTENTS

Introduction ix

Chapter 1   The Me of Tomorrow 1
Chapter 2   A Balanced Life 25
Chapter 3   Learning for Life 47
Chapter 4   Relationships of Tomorrow 78
Chapter 5   Me @ Work: Building a Valuable Career 118
Chapter 6   Your Wealth of Tomorrow 142
Chapter 7   Reaching Tomorrow 170
Chapter 8   Building Your Strategy 210

Epilogue 229
Bibliography 231
Acknowledgments 235
About the Author 237

INTRODUCTION

This book is a personal-planning manual. It introduces you to some fascinating people you will get to know well. These people are your future selves—your *future me*s: your mes of tomorrow five, ten, fifteen, and twenty years from now. Hopefully, you'll also get to know me, the author. However, starting out, you may be asking, "How did this passion for planning get started?"

Growing up in the beautiful but economically fragile country of Panama, I wanted nothing more than to be an engineer. I don't recall any particular attraction to the vocation itself. Honestly, I wasn't especially driven to build or create. My rationale was simple: I knew that in Panama engineers made a good living. I just wanted to achieve that apparently comfortable life.

Not by coincidence, my best friend from my teenage school days shared my ambition. At a time and in a place where prospects were uncertain, we sometimes talked about having secure jobs and better lives. We lived across the road from another friend, whose dad was an engineer at the power company. Unlike ours, this friend's family regularly traveled abroad on vacation. We found this idea extremely exciting. By the time we were fourteen, my friend and I were convinced that becoming an engineer was the most worthwhile ambition.

But there was one slight problem. We were still more than a year away from starting high school—grades ten through twelve. And the only visible path to fulfilling this cherished dream flowed through the high school science track. This track was the most competitive and challenging by far, and it was adjudicated at the end of ninth grade. To get accepted, we would need excellent math and science scores from our ninth-grade work.

My friend and I were both aware of the challenge. We both had a full year to prepare. I vividly remember discussing how we needed to think ahead and make sure we studied hard. Neither of us wanted our dreams of becoming engineers dashed at the very first hurdle. Getting the best math and science scores became my obsession. I started visualizing the consequences of failure—how it would feel when the results came in at the end of the year. This became my primary preoccupation and a powerful motivation. I thought of little else. As I immersed myself in math and science to the exclusion of almost everything else, those grades became my sole focus.

By contrast, my friend didn't obsess about those grades like I did. He was confident and unworried and never visualized his future feelings when the results were announced, as far as I could tell. He paid no particular attention to his progress over the following year. So at the end of the year, when the results came out, only one of us got the grades and entered the cherished science track. You guessed it: that obsessive planner—me! Back when I neared the end of eighth grade, that visualization exercise—imagining how I would feel without that place in the high school science track—had been the perfect motivator. Envisaging how that me of more than a year later would feel had provided just the incentive I needed.

The lesson I took from this lasted much longer than my ambition to become an engineer. Thinking ahead and planning what I needed to do to reach a goal appeared simple and obvious. Some other students behaved the same way. But I was staggered at how the vast majority lived in the moment and didn't plan at all. From this point, planning and visualizing the future became a lifelong habit of mine. At so many junctures throughout high school and college, I found myself thinking about not only the best choice for that moment but, more important, the best choice for the long term. I became someone who played the long game.

As time went by, I extended this planning habit beyond study to almost every area of my life. Over the years, I shared many of my life-planning ideas with friends. Much later, when I was the father of teenagers, I continued studying and developing models to show them how planning ahead leads to a better life. For example, my wife and I made sure our children played a sport year-round. We made it a family rule because I believe sports teach many valuable lessons. To give our children control, my wife and I told them they could change their sport every year if they wanted—as long as they chose one.

Many friends and colleagues appreciated my ideas. Even the most impulsive, happy-go-lucky friends seemed to enjoy them, and we engaged in many healthy debates. At least it got them thinking about tomorrow. Several started to nag me to organize my thoughts and write a book. That became *The Me of Tomorrow*.

As I've grown older, I've come to understand that the most precious nonrenewable resource in life is time. It is so priceless that I became driven to manage it more effectively. Of course, planning itself takes time, but my process taught me over and over again that front-end planning always saves me time on the back end. Planning became my ultimate time-saver. My hope with this book is to help other people learn what it took me many years to understand. Simply put, I want to help people save time.

And so to those fascinating future people. If you follow some of my advice, all your future mes will thank your me of today for helping to make their lives so much more fulfilling and for saving them so much time. For most of us, today's pressurized world, with its myriad distractions and challenges, relegates planning for our future mes to the bottom of our to-do lists. Occasionally, in rare stolen moments, we dream of the future—but rather vaguely. We rarely plan for it. Most of us allow life's conveyor belt to accelerate past, distributing its pains and pleasures. We make decisions for today with limited forethought. Like my old schoolmate and like so many friends and acquaintances I've encountered through the years, many of us don't think systematically about how today's decisions will make life better tomorrow.

This book will teach you how to think and plan rigorously for the future. My frameworks and exercises might make you feel like a business planner. But the planning will be yours and yours alone. It will tell you not what to think but how. However, I will also dispense a little advice about the *what*—some hard-won wisdom that has worked for me. *The Me of Tomorrow* is a how-to guide to set yourself up for future happiness. It shows how me-of-tomorrow thinking can influence every aspect of your life: balance, personal development, relationships, finance, career, health, and self-confidence.

Many of these ideas have been buzzing around in my head for more than twenty years. As a first-generation immigrant from humble beginnings, I have always been an observer of people and a sponge for ideas. I trust data more than I do opinions and test different theories and approaches until I find one that solves the problem best. Over my business career, I have coached and mentored hundreds of people along their personal-growth journeys. I have synthesized ideas from colleagues, authors, students, and friends who helped me plan for my many tomorrows. Many of these ideas I learned and adapted from them.

The first people to hear many of these ideas were my two children. As any other dad trying to be the best father I could be, I shared with them as soon as they could understand. Even when they were teenagers, these ideas made sense to them. Today, they are in their early twenties, and they realize now more than ever the relevance of these ideas. When I shared with them the various chapters of this book, they said to me, "Dad, we already know all of that. We have heard it from you all our lives."

I believe that the earlier you start to use me-of-tomorrow thinking, the better. It becomes valuable once you've struck out on your own and assumed the responsibilities and challenges that come with young adulthood and early career progression. The younger you start, the more planning runway you have.

However, I also believe it's never too late to plan. I plan and replan avidly for my me of tomorrow. It's always fulfilling to scan life's domains and plan for the future. This planning is worthwhile whether you're early in your career, relationships, and personal development, seeking guidance and direction, or long into your path but looking to recalibrate. Planning beats dreaming, and it's just as exciting. I hope the book's ideas provide as much food for thought as they have me over many fulfilling years.

CHAPTER 1
THE ME OF TOMORROW

Tomorrow belongs to those who can hear it coming.
—DAVID BOWIE

Tomorrow is a thief of pleasure.
—REX HARRISON

Although I conceived this book much earlier, I finally wrote it, after years of gestation, in 2020, during the COVID-19 pandemic. While cheerfully writing about life planning, I couldn't help but see the irony. Of all the pandemic's many casualties, maybe we could add the frustration of so many plans. The pandemic threw everything up in the air. People canceled weddings, vacations, business trips—in fact, many jettisoned almost all their careful designs for 2020. So many of us changed not just what to plan but how to plan. It was hard to prepare for the week ahead, let alone the next twenty years. How could planning for the future carry any meaning during a time of shaken foundations and uncertainty?

After reflecting on this question, I had a different thought. The world quickly discovered that people differed in their risk profiles vis-à-vis the virus. Generally, although not exclusively, people in better health and with robust immune systems fared better than those with preexisting health conditions. Although the severity of the sickness sometimes appeared random, statistically, a healthy immune system was a huge benefit. The idea occurred to me: Did these healthier people gain that advantage because they had planned their lives better than others had? Did this better planning cause them less disruption when compared to others?

For me, thinking about the me of tomorrow far predates the virus. It has become second nature, essential to creating a meaningful life. It's my bread and butter. However, paradoxically, understanding how to plan in the age of coronavirus took on an even greater meaning.

Our sense of balance; thirst for knowledge; and approach to health, career, finances, and relationships required even more forethought and attention than ever before. Envisaging future tomorrows puts us in a better position to deal with today. At some point, we knew the planet's current nightmare would end and an unpredictable "new normal" would emerge.

Having the mental discipline to envisage a different life and a different life stage makes us smarter, more adaptable, and more conscious of our choices every day. This book is all about decision-making; COVID-19 just made us consider our daily decisions with another unknown variable. It reinforced my belief that planning, both past and present, holds meaning and resonance in times of stress and greatest uncertainty, just as it does when life seems more normal. Unpredictability is part of life.

ME-OF-TOMORROW THINKING

I wrote this manual because I believe many of us will benefit from thinking differently about how we make decisions and prioritize our lives.

How often do you stop and think, *How will today's decisions help me tomorrow?* Or, think of this another way: How much time do you spend searching for a way of doing something or approaching a problem? Think of the times you can't find a piece of information you remember using before. How often do we reinvent the wheel in business and in life?

As one example, I remember as a young manager developing a new process for training my team. I thought it would get great results. However, shortly after starting, I abandoned it. I realized it would take a ton of effort. *My team is small—won't it be faster just to wing it?* Sure, we saved time and effort in the short term, but I wasn't thinking about the next year and the year after, when there would be fifty people to train.

To take an even simpler example: How many times did someone recommend you a plumber or a car mechanic but, when the time came for you to get a quote for a necessary repair, you couldn't remember the source or the service provider? Instead of saving the number to your phone and labeling it *plumber*, you didn't take the time. In every example, both large and small, meaningful or trivial, the essence of the problem is this failure to consider what I call the *me of tomorrow*. The me of today was satisfied, but the me of tomorrow was not remotely considered. A few seconds of activity by the me of today would have saved the me of tomorrow minutes or hours.

Just to be clear: this book is *not* about failing to seize the moment. It is about developing a mental framework to give those future mes a seat at the decision-making table, especially concerning important choices. It's about getting into the habit of making the me of today plan, consequently making the me of tomorrow's life easier and more fulfilled. It's about developing the discipline and the habit of considering the me of tomorrow much more than most of us do today.

I'm not telling you *not* to live life to the fullest; life is about experiencing wonder and joy, which is essential. But a new planning discipline—me-of-tomorrow thinking—will help you realize the much greater joy and success throughout your whole life.

AVOIDING REGRETS

One of my biggest inspirations to write this book is actually a sad one. As I've grown older, I've come across many people who, though outwardly successful in business and life, suffer from stress and worry, guilt and shame, financial problems, and career stalemate. I have seen that if they excel in one area, their shortcomings in another really bother them. In my opinion, much of this suffering—lost jobs, failed marriages, financial stress—is avoidable. It can be traced to one simple flaw in almost every case: the failure to envisage their mes of tomorrow when facing many important decisions. Most of us make key decisions without thinking about the broader impact of those important decisions.

This chapter explains why it matters, even in today's world, which seems laser focused on maximizing today's pleasure. It provides you with practical exercises to change your habits as you make life decisions both large and small.

As I reflect on my own life, I realize the sheer number of ideas those former mes should have considered. I wish I could go back and tell them how to plan and make decisions. This book explains and demonstrates what's involved in developing a me-of-tomorrow habit. This habit does not inhibit today's opportunities but gives your future me so many more options and a more abundant life. It will help you accelerate your learning so you can live in the moment and capture life but simultaneously consider what that your future me would want you to do. It will also help you save that most precious resource: time.

Life is beautiful and complex, with so many variables and changes. Living to your full potential demands planning. Think of this planning not as complicated, joy-deadening analysis but as positive visualization and dreaming, just in a simple, consistent way. In this book, I share ideas of me-of-tomorrow thinking in key areas of life, chapter by chapter.

Use it for your life as you would a manual for your car. It will help you understand the maintenance you need to do and the tools you need to fix many life problems. Your future me will thank your present me every single day. If you follow some of these suggestions, both mes—today's and tomorrow's—will live more-fulfilling and ultimately happier lives.

UNDERSTANDING THE ME OF TOMORROW

Everything starts with understanding how this type of thinking can help you. By acknowledging and merely paying attention to your future me in decision-making, your tomorrows will be more comfortable and fulfilling. Nothing else you do will add more to the quality of life than this simple habit does. Appreciating this spans all aspects of life and helps not just individuals but businesses and institutions too.

"Tomorrow never comes" is one of life's oldest truisms. It alerts us to the pressing urgency of now; it tells us to do what's right in front of us, because when tomorrow arrives, it becomes today, and tomorrow then becomes yet another day. But thinking deeply about tomorrow is critical because life without planning is a life of chaos and a life without dreaming and imagining the future is drab and sterile.

The quotes from David Bowie and Rex Harrison at the beginning of this chapter illustrate two different perspectives on the future. Balancing today and tomorrow—acting and planning—is one of life's greatest challenges and requires us to keep tomorrow at the front of our minds today in every step we take and every decision we make. It also means having the discipline to plan and envisage the future and, in doing so, make better decisions today. This might sound exhausting, but this type of planning can rapidly become a habit and improve your life, career, relationships, and mental and physical health. Once I started it, me-of-tomorrow planning slowly but surely became second nature. That doesn't mean I am perfect, but I am more aware of what the future me would want. I give him a seat at the decision-making table. This chapter will explore this idea in greater depth. How do we change what we do now to keep the future top of mind, listening to what's coming, but also prevent tomorrow from becoming that thief of pleasure?

At the end of the chapter, I will share some simple exercises that can help you start to embed me-of-tomorrow thinking into everyday life. But first, let's tackle some of the illusions that make me-of-tomorrow thinking seem so difficult.

CARPE DIEM—SEIZE THE DAY!

The suddenness and often random nature of traumatic events remind us that life is short. We hear heartbreaking tales of successful, diligent people who never reap the fruits of their labor. After lifetimes of work and sacrifice, they suffer fatal illnesses just as they realize their visions or begin their well-earned retirement. In the span of eighteen months, two of the most senior leaders at one of my employers passed in their early sixties after very successful professional careers. Both of them were so painfully close to their retirement. This was unfortunate on so many levels.

We also know of hardworking parents who miss seminal moments in their children's lives and then spend years regretting it, wishing they had prioritized these events over their dedication to work. This is the reality of modern life: people sacrificing their health, family life, or relationships because they do what seems to be the right thing for that very moment. Life sometimes gives us early lessons in regrets, too, if we care to notice.

I have a particularly poignant memory of one such lesson. As a teenager, I visited my grandmother's grave with my dad. We left two dozen roses at her headstone. Soon after we left, my dad turned to me and said, "I wish I'd bought her flowers more often when she was alive."

Many of my younger friends in their twenties struggle with committing time to their parents as they live their busy lives—after all, they only went through the process of separation a few years ago.

But as time passes, their parents sometimes get sick and pass away, and the children then have to live with guilt and regret. The lesson I learned is to do things for loved ones while they are alive and can enjoy them. This is about both living in the present and also thinking about the future. Do good things now: it's essential both for the me of today and also so the me of tomorrow won't experience regret.

Stories like these can have a powerful effect on us. In today's frantic and unpredictable world, we are acutely conscious that life is rushing by and can be wiped away in a microsecond. This causes us to internalize a straightforward message: carpe diem—seize the day!

This message affects our behavior and our decision-making in matters great and small. How many times have we seized that massive piece of chocolate cake? Or that third or fourth glass of wine? Or that fifth or sixth beer? Or a double bacon cheeseburger when really a single would do? These don't feel like consequential decisions, but by seizing these moments, we are spellbound by that drumbeat; we grab that cake, wine, beer, or burger because the moment for pleasure is *now*. Once in my career, I witnessed a very high-potential young executive lose his job because he'd had one too many drinks at the company Christmas party and acted inappropriately under the influence. Everyone liked him and thought he didn't mean any harm, but the company had to take action or risk future liability.

Many decisions become almost immediate regrets. We wind up wishing we had thought things through more carefully. Continuing with these simple examples, we just end up feeling too full, having headaches, and suffering from bad hangovers. In extreme cases, maybe our quick decisions cause something much more consequential, like a DWI. The reason we make such decisions—some momentous, some trivial—is simple. The me of today beats the me of tomorrow. That first me rules us. We lack the foresight to imagine a future me telling the current me what to do. This is a failure of imagination, and it's something I've been working through all my life.

EAT, DRINK, AND BE MERRY, FOR TOMORROW YOU DIE!

This mash-up of two biblical verses has never seemed more relevant than now.[1] It feels tailor-made for today's millennial generation, who famously values experiences over material things. Our desire to experience is driven in part by the fear and uncertainty of ultramodern life, the speed of change, and our searing daily experiences.

We are bombarded with headlines of impending doom: climate change, terrorism, mass shootings, coronavirus, antibiotic-resistant infections, political turmoil, racial strife. Some political leaders stoke fear and anger as motivational tools. And the media's relentless clickbait focus usually points us to more bad news.

It's true, of course, that tomorrow isn't promised to anyone. However, for most of us, the odds are there will be many tomorrows. For much of the world, life has never been better, especially for those lucky enough to live in countries with modern medicine, adequate nutrition, and strong institutions to protect their citizenry. Boil them down, and many of our daily fears and concerns are what some would call *first-world problems*.[2] Most of us have the basics covered: food, shelter, energy, water—perhaps even broadband and an unlimited data plan.

For the vast majority of us, tomorrows will flow. In fact, for nearly all of us, many more of those tomorrows. In 1900, US life expectancy at birth was around forty-seven years. By 1950, it had surged to sixty-eight, and for those born in the 1980s, it's in the midseventies. We can safely expect today's college students to have an excellent chance of waking up in the 2080s or even in the next century.

Across the globe, despite the pressing problems we hear about every day, most more consequential than our first-world ones, average life expectancy actually increased by five and a half years

---

[1] Ecclesiastes 8:15, "Then I commended mirth, because a man hath no better thing under the sun, than to eat, and to drink, and to be merry," and Isaiah 22:13, "Let us eat and drink; for tomorrow we shall die."

[2] Attributed to G. K. Payne's essay in a 1979 issue of the journal *Built Environment*.

between 2000 and 2016—the fastest increase since the 1960s. And this is before the anticipated wave of genetically based medicines come onstream. The evidence is clear: we need to think about the me of tomorrow because, for the overwhelming majority of us, there will be many tomorrows to plan for.

Of course, life is more about quality than quantity. For most of us, as we get older, our material circumstances improve. And unless you're one of those people lucky enough to be born into wealth, our perspective changes. As we advance in our jobs and careers, prosperity creeps on us. It's hard to remember how I felt when I was juggling bills or wondering how to pay my rent, but that was my *today* for many years. When there's more money around and more possible choices about how to spend it, we tend to think planning for the future doesn't matter anymore. But nothing could be further from the truth.

HARDWIRED FOR TODAY

Our future selves are strangers to us. Studies have shown that when we try to picture ourselves in the future, those new mes becomes unrecognizable. Consequently, we can't correctly envisage that future state, that me of tomorrow. A large body of work in human psychology has validated this phenomenon.

This kind of thinking has a demonstrated basis in neuroscience. The less you feel an affinity to the other person, the less active the medial prefrontal cortex seems to be.[3] As UCLA psychologist Hal Hirschfield noted, "Why would you save money for your future self when, to your brain, it feels like you're just handing away your money to a complete stranger?"[4]

In 2017, the **Institute for the Future,** based in Palo Alto, California, published an attitudinal research study that explored

---

[3] Pengmin Qin, Georg Northoff, "How Is Our Self Related to Midline Regions and the Default-Mode Network?," *NeuroImage* 57, no. 3 (2011): 1221–33.
[4] Quoted by Cynthia Lee, UCLA Newsroom, 2015.

how people think about their own and society's future.[5] It found that most Americans rarely or never think about something that might happen in thirty years. More than one-third rarely or never envisage something they might do ten years from now. The furthest tomorrow that people can imagine is five years from now: three of four people can do that. Hence that classic interview question, Where do you see yourself five years from now?

But even that 75 percent admitted they only give the five-year future a thought once or twice per month. As I'll discuss in more detail, this focus on today over tomorrow has serious real-world consequences for us all. Conversely, training ourselves to focus on tomorrow has incredible benefits.

COGNITIVE FAILURES

In addition to these neurological failings, a series of what psychologists call *cognitive failures* also conspire to make today seem much more appealing than tomorrow. First, there is constant social pressure to maximize pleasure, have a good time, eat, drink, and be merry. The tendency toward focusing on today over tomorrow is powerful.

Unfortunately, for some people, me-of-today thinking is driven by the seeming impossibility of reaching a happy tomorrow. Economic issues like crushing higher-education debt and high housing costs often make the idea of a prosperous tomorrow hard to picture. Together, forty-five million Americans owe more than $1.5 trillion in student loan debt, and each recent graduate owes, on average, almost $30,000. Even the average professional can't afford market rents in places like New York City and San Francisco. If you're in that boat, it's hard to think about a future life with a spouse, children, and dogs. It's as if our minds tell us tomorrow is so uncertain that we can't think about it until we dig out from today's problems.

These problems are far from universal, but even if that sounds like you, I would argue that these kinds of challenges make it even

---

[5] IFFF, the American Future Gap Survey, 2017.

more useful and even more exciting to do some me-of-tomorrow thinking and imagining.

Surprising as it sounds, every preceding generation suffered from similar fears and foreboding, often for different reasons. In many cases, the challenges were more severe and the outlook more uncertain. Today may have its problems, but ignoring tomorrow doesn't make it any easier.

Over the last few decades, social psychologists and behavioral economists have reinvented the science of decision-making. Far from being the rational thinkers that traditional economic models assumed, human beings consistently display apparently irrational behavior when making decisions, especially economic ones. Richard Posner, a leading American legal scholar and economist, believes what he calls these "cognitive quirks" are explained by evolutionary biology. Adam Smith—often called the father of economics—talked about passions being myopic; other economists called it a failure of willpower.

Of course, many of these failures have nothing to do with time. Still, economist Paul Samuelson called "intertemporal choice" one such failure. Samuelson's theory of intertemporal choice held that people discount future consumption, although not in a consistent way. Psychologist Richard Thaler talked about the "present bias," the phenomenon whereby people are much more inclined to value a win now rather than a win later. He demonstrated that people are not as controlled, smart, and forward thinking as the classical economic models imply. He recalled once discussing these so-called rational economic models with a room of psychologists, who all fell about laughing! The fact is that each of us is actually two people at the same time: a planner and a doer—and the planner often loses out to the doer.[6] So planning for the future does not come naturally to any of us.

Thinking about the me of tomorrow is even more challenging when we're young. Psychologists teach us that the frontal lobe is not

---

[6] Richard H. Thaler, *Misbehaving: The Making of Behavioral Economics* (New York: W.W. Norton, 2015).

fully formed until we are twenty-five years old, so thinking ahead is incredibly difficult before then.

Even after twenty-five, it's not easy. I recall reading *The 7 Habits of Highly Effective People* in my late twenties.[7] I liked how Stephen Covey told us to live our lives according to what we would want others to remember and say about us at our funeral. However, remembering to think of this in the abstract is well-nigh impossible when we are faced with life's multitudinous decisions.

Even then, I realized that I needed to build a framework to systematically think about tomorrow today. I will propose such a framework later in this chapter.

KEEPING UP WITH THE JONESES

Human beings are social creatures. Whatever our circumstances, we compare ourselves with people we think of as peers. Although we like to deny it, this is the classic *keeping up with the Joneses* effect. For many people, the laser focus on today over tomorrow is shaped by the people around us. It is this lack of independent thinking and decision-making that makes us most vulnerable to mistakes that ignore the future.

One interesting error we all make is the tendency to think our peers are as rich as the things we see they have. Actually, when we look over the fence at our neighbors, we see what they *spend*, not what they *have*. I know of many people in beautiful "wealthy" neighborhoods who spend way above their means. Their cars and vacations are financed by credit or—as in some cases I know personally—by their parents. They don't really *have* the money to live as they do, but they sure *spend* as though they do. I'll talk much more about this in chapter 6.

Keeping up with the Joneses starts earlier than we can even imagine. Whether it's the type of phone our kids ask for in middle school, the

---

[7] Stephen R. Covey, *The 7 Habits of Highly Effective People: Powerful Lessons in Personal Change*, 25th anniversary ed. (New York: Simon & Schuster, 2013).

make of car they want in high school, or the name of the college they wish to attend, social pressure is more often than not *the* key driver. Middle or high schoolers don't have a frame of reference for the utility or relative value of cars or phones. They certainly don't see how it will impact their mes of tomorrow. At that age, that's the furthest thing from their underdeveloped minds. Social context is everything. But think of the habit that's teaching and what frame of reference their impressionable minds ingest. No wonder keeping up with the Joneses becomes a defining characteristic of their future behavior.

VISUALIZING THE ME OF TOMORROW

The opportunity we all have is to give more voting power to the me of tomorrow. To give those future mes a seat at the table. Throughout this book, I talk about how decisions and specific behaviors—taken with the tomorrow in mind—help in so many ways. I look at learning, career pathing, leadership, relationships, and health. But first, here are some examples of solid me-of-tomorrow thinking.

One of my favorites is in the area of career development. As a career coach, I've come across this often. Let's say that you are installed in a good company with good prospects. You are performing well in your field. There's a natural tendency to push for a promotion. You deserve it: you've mastered your job, and you're contributing more than your less-experienced peers—perhaps you're even training them. Then, an opportunity for the next level up comes up, but it is not in your current function. The learning-and-development team wants you, and they know just the way to entice you: with a promotion. A promotion typically comes with more responsibility, a better title, and, crucially, more money. The me of today is excited and satisfied.

But think for a minute about the me of tomorrow: Will your me of tomorrow want to be at a higher and higher level in that kind of job function? That career path identifies you as a respected specialist—an expert. Think about your career path more broadly: In this company and industry, where do senior executives and business decision-makers come from? For example, if it's a technology company, the senior leadership team members are unlikely to come from the learning-and-development department. If you want to reach the top, doesn't it make more sense to think of other functions that are core to the company's mission? Maybe the me of tomorrow would tell you to forgo that promotion and instead move laterally into a function that the company and industry really value, perhaps marketing, sales, or engineering. In that situation, thinking about the future me could cause you to decline that deserved promotion and bide your time until a more promising opportunity presents itself. I'll discuss this more in chapter 5.

Another simple example is the decision to buy a new car. Perhaps you have the option of a European model with all the bells and whistles. You have two toddlers, so college is something far off in the dim and distant future. You'll worry about that later. Obviously, you rationalize, you'll be making more money then. Sitting at the dealership, you're not fast enough to do the math: What would saving $100 or $200 in the monthly payment do to your college savings account—assuming you have one? You don't think that the me of tomorrow ten to twelve years hence may suffer sleepless nights worrying about how to pay for college. How many fights with your spouse would you avoid by saving better? That me of tomorrow would want you to step out of the Mercedes dealership and head right across the street to the Toyota or Honda dealership. How much difference would it make if you invested the savings in an S&P 500 index fund? A $200-per-month saving over the last fifteen years would now be worth more than $83,000. The same argument applies if you are single and living in an apartment. Perhaps, in that case, the me of tomorrow would have preferred you begin saving sooner for a down payment on a home.

The same applies to clothing. As I discuss in chapter 8, we all need our armor. When we wake up every morning, we need that edge to give us the confidence to get through the day. For some people, it's a state of mind—a game face; for others, it might be the clothes they wear and the image they project. If clothes provide confidence, they're essential. Every season, we may buy new clothes because we believe we deserve to look good. We buy a $1,300 Giorgio Armani jacket for $650 because it is on sale. We buy shoes, watches, leather handbags, and gloves in colors to match the many clothes we own. We do this repeatedly, for every summer and fall, for twenty-five years.

One day, we may lose our job and need savings to bridge us to the next one, only to find that there's nothing in the kitty. Our lives of new clothes, restaurants, and travel have eaten away any systematic approach to savings. But the me of fifty years old would have liked to have a serious talk with the me of thirty years old. Of course, looking good is important, but that fifty-year-old me would have appreciated if the thirty-year-old me had been more careful, didn't buy new clothes every season, didn't dine out all the time, and didn't charge vacations to a credit card. Just a quick check-in with the me of twenty years' time will avoid a world of hurt.

The reality is that for the vast majority of us, whatever age we are, there's a tomorrow that holds financial requirements, health requirements, and relationship requirements. Most of the time, our me-of-today decisions are quick and straightforward: What should I wear today? What do I want for lunch? These decisions usually—although not always—have little to do with fulfilling our dreams. However, every now and then, the decisions we face are not so inconsequential: Should I take that job or not? What vehicle should I buy? How we approach these critical decisions will have a massive impact on the me of tomorrow. These situations demand that we not only think about the me of today but think in a disciplined way about how different decisions will impact the me of tomorrow. In my experience, the most impactful decisions are the ones where we would most benefit from asking, "What would the me of tomorrow would want me to do?" or "What would the me of next year want me to do?"

I recently took my daughter and her friends on a trip to the beach. They were going out with some friends one night, and I discussed this in the context of both drinking and driving and drinking in general. I told them two things:

- Your me of tomorrow wouldn't want you to drive if you drank too much.
- Your me of literal tomorrow wouldn't want you to drink so much that you don't enjoy the beach and instead of have a hangover and miss the morning sun.

It's hard to tell college students anything. However, just raising the ideas had a surprising and immediate effect. One of them told me, "The me of Monday next week will want me to spend a few hours working on an essay due Tuesday." Imagine my surprise! If this becomes a habit, it's compelling and life affirming.

The urgent need for me-of-tomorrow thinking applies just as readily to business leaders too. Short-term thinking permeates the higher echelons of business, especially the obsession with quarterly results and the perverse incentives that often drive this behavior.

But it applies away from the boardroom too. Serious business planning is often neglected and replaced with projects that address an immediate need. When processes break down, we usually jump to build one. Still, far too often, they're made to solve today's problems, not the issues of tomorrow. They won't scale, they don't account for technology changes, and they just put bandages on the issue. A year or two later, businesses find themselves addressing the same problem again.

IT'S NOT ALL ABOUT MONEY

As some of these examples show, it's easy to think of me-of-tomorrow thinking purely in the context of money. Obviously, forgone consumption now will make the future more secure and comfortable. But contrary to what we are generally led to believe, more expensive things don't make us happier. Part of this comes down to psychological tricks our minds play. Many of the cognitive failures identified by social psychologists show how such biases permeate our thinking. For example, what Richard Thaler calls the "endowment effect" demonstrates that we value things we own more than those we don't, even if the actual economic value is opposite.[8]

We also ignore sunk costs and value items inconsistently. And as Bernoulli's risk-aversion theory proposes, the rate of increase in our perceived utility declines as we get wealthier. Forgoing current consumption to benefit the me of tomorrow might not be as painful as we think. Daniel Kahneman, Nobel Prize–winning author of *Thinking, Fast and Slow*, describes how losses hurt us twice as much as gains make us feel good.[9] The lesson I take from this finding is clear: the pain the me of tomorrow will feel from an unplanned decision is much greater than the pain the me of today feels now. It's also been well established that we experience life through changes: we observe change but not the status quo.

Cognitive failures aside, it's simply true that consumption now doesn't buy happiness, especially when compared with the real challenges the me of tomorrow could face because of current profligacy. Avoiding the temptation to keep up with the Joneses makes much less difference to our current happiness or sense of well-being than we think.

PLANNING FOR THE ME OF TOMORROW

Our usual irrational selves are not wired, either psychologically or socially, to prioritize decisions that affect us in the future, especially one that's very hard to picture. But developing a framework for incorporating me-of-tomorrow thinking into today's decisions and making it a regular habit is not difficult. Once you have a framework, it will become second nature. I consider the framework almost every day and in virtually every decision I make.

---

[8] Richard H. Thaler, *Misbehaving: The Making of Behavioral Economics* (New York: W.W. Norton, 2015).
[9] Daniel Kahneman, *Thinking, Fast and Slow* (New York: Farrar, Straus and Giroux, 2013).

The most significant change we need is a psychological one: a new mindset. At first, this might require clearing your head, scheduling time on a lazy Saturday afternoon, and reflecting on your life and where you are in your journey. Let your dreams flow and your thoughts contend. Once you've mastered the thinking, it's something you'll consider every day. I find it helpful to use a matrix that looks like this (figure 1).

	Me in my thirties	Me in my forties	Me in my fifties	Me in my sixties
Professional				
Family				
Health				
Community				
Economic				
Spiritual				

Figure 1.

In this matrix, develop a statement for the blank cells. Planning experts will tell you that goals must be measurable, but in this exercise, the most important thing is to develop the habit. In your first pass through the matrix, you can be as descriptive as you like, but try hard to visualize. It's fun—plus the quality of your answers and the depth of your thinking will grow. This is a warmup exercise for the planning we will undertake in chapter 8.

If you are in your twenties, you should fill in as much of the matrix as your imagination will allow. Although it's challenging to envision so far ahead, that's all part of the fun. Older readers should just focus on their tomorrows—their future mes. Of course, you could subdivide the decades and create five- and even two-year plans. It all depends on where you are in your life journey.

Your statements should be as specific as you feel comfortable with, and the format should be "In my thirties, I want to …" Note that something vague like "have more money in the bank" as an economic goal is less helpful than something like "be at level 3 on the wealth scale in chapter 6." Similarly, a stronger professional statement like "be at a director level in a fast-growing company" is better than "be promoted." A family statement might be "have my children playing sports and thriving at school."

As you complete the matrix, it's worthwhile thinking about the negatives too. What would be a bad situation or outcome? Psychology tells us that imagining something negative can be a good motivator for behavioral change. If it helps, use parents, grandparents, and older people you know as proxies for your future self. But your proxy doesn't have to be someone you know well. For example, on the professional side, you can look at LinkedIn, find someone from the same background or school and with the same degree as yours, and see where that person is now. Your matrix might have different elements and, of course, different timelines, depending on where you are in your life journey.

This book was the direct consequence of me-of-tomorrow planning. Before I turned fifty, I did some planning for the me of age seventy. Having seen the satisfaction my own father got from becoming an author later in life, I concluded the me of seventy would also enjoy the satisfaction of having compiled some of his life learnings into a book. Once it was on my list, I went to work on it.

In the next chapter, I will discuss the different mes—the essential elements of life and how to balance them. Later in the book, I provide planning tools for tracking your personal finances, managing relationships, and even optimizing your health. But first, start with the areas of your life you think are most essential and which are the easiest to visualize. Picture that me of tomorrow, and think about what success looks like in your chosen time frame. Then, before finishing the exercise, add another row (figure 2).

	Me in my thirties	Me in my forties	Me in my fifties	Me in my sixties
Trade-offs				

Figure 2.

Only once you finish the exercise will you be ready to understand that you'll have trade-offs. If you focus on one area of your life, something else in your life will be impacted. This is something we will discuss in more detail in chapter 2.

Once you've built your me-of-tomorrow matrix, think about how today's decisions might change the trajectory. For example, would taking an additional class or degree impact the professional or economic circumstances of the me of ten years from now?

Although timelines vary, this approach works even for people in mid or late career. One professional I know looked deeply at his current skills and expertise at age fifty. Knowing he would need to command a continual high income at age sixty and sixty-five, and understanding the latent ageism that affects older workers, he made an expensive and time-consuming decision. He decided to improve his skills with a master's degree in an emerging related discipline. Having this additional and highly valued string to his bow acted as insurance against being cast adrift. At the same time, it offered him different career-path options to protect against being sidelined in his current role.

ADVANCED TOPICS: YOUR LEGACY

Scott Mautz, business leader and author, recalled a reply Apple CEO Tim Cook gave when asked, "When you think about yourself, what is your highest value?"[10] It's a difficult question. After a slight pause and an explanation of his lifetime search for purpose, Tim Cook shared it in one compelling sentence: "And at some point, you recognize the reason we are all here is to help somebody else—that is the sole reason we are here." He went on to add, "You're here in service of other people. It's not about you."

Mautz also mentioned a speech from Fred Rogers of *Mister Rogers' Neighborhood*. Rogers asked those in his audience to close their

---

[10] Scott Mautz, *Find the Fire: Ignite Your Inspiration—and Make Work Exciting Again* (New York: AMACOM, American Management Association, 2017).

eyes and think about someone in their lives who made a profound difference in the people they'd grown to be.

This exercise raises the questions of legacy. Ask yourself, "When asked the same question, who would think of me? Who would think of me as having made a profound difference in their lives?"

If you're at the life stage when you've started to think about this, try adding another column to your me-of-tomorrow matrix—*my legacy*. Try thinking about your legacy across all these domains. Think of who will want to mention you and what you would like for them to say.

BECOME AN INFORMATION HOG

One of the other critical habits that helps you realize the promise of me of tomorrow thinking is devouring, collecting, and storing information. In chapter 3, I discuss lifetime learning. As Gandhi said (while not necessarily channeling me-of-tomorrow thinking), "Live as if you were to die tomorrow. Learn as if you were to live forever."

Having an information-retention mindset is a critical skill. I mentioned earlier a simple example regarding phone numbers. But that's just the tip of the iceberg. Over the last twenty years, I have developed—through trial and error at times and through many spins of the technology wheel—a system to hog information. The principle is simple: when the me of today finds valuable information, I instantly double or triple its value by thinking about how the me of tomorrow could use it. Then I store it in a system designed for easy retention. This process doesn't have to be complicated.

I started to adopt this habit reasonably early in life, once I had absorbed the universal truth that the only nonrenewable asset in life is time. Now I try to give myself a mental nudge whenever I know I am wasting time. When I recognize that my current activity is unproductive, uninteresting, or unlikely to yield a future benefit to me or others, I try to move quickly to the next activity. And one of the most obvious time wasters is reinventing the wheel. When it dawned on me that I had squandered too much time looking for information that had once been at my fingertips, I became motivated to develop a filtering mechanism to save me time in the future. My current approach is a simple hierarchical one.

- I store simple information (recipes, plumbers' phone numbers, license plate numbers, frequent-flier numbers, etc.) in Google Keep. Note that tools like Apple Notes and Microsoft OneNote work the same way, and there are also paid versions, such as Evernote.
- If I find something useful in a magazine or newspaper, like a cool way to present information or a recipe or compelling quotation, I take a cell phone picture and add to that information store.
- I have a folder in my information store for every job I have ever had (with the title of the job or company). Every time I work on a critical new project or develop a new process, I store my frameworks and new thinking in slides or documents (obviously excluding anything proprietary). I upload them to my store and categorize them by the role I had. When I need to reuse something, I remember it by that role.
- My information store is divided by function: finance, HR, marketing, sales, strategy, and so forth. Because much of my career has been in sales and marketing, I also have subdivisions within these functions, such as product marketing, marketing communications, positioning, presales, solution selling and channel, and the like.
- When I read or listen to a particularly impactful book (see chapter 3), I sit down, write three or four pages of notes, and add to my data store's relevant section. I have found that I retain the information easiest if I do this after reading one or two chapters. This is under a folder called *Books*.
- I categorize all my disparate information in a system like the me-of-tomorrow matrix: professional, family, health, financial, and so on. Information for a specific future-use

period is labeled with that year. I'll talk more about the matrix in chapter 2.
- Each of my folders rolls up to a cloud information store—in my case, OneDrive, but Google Drive or iCloud works as well. For the longest time, I have called the master folder *valuable stuff*. Periodically I archive information to my cloud file store. This activity also serves as a way to refresh my mind of the most recent new learning.

An increasing body of research also suggests that keeping a diary has extraordinary benefits in terms of reduced stress, better planning, and improved memory. The act of writing each entry focuses the mind beyond the here and now to thoughts, dreams, and plans for the future—the me of tomorrow. Some professionals believe it doesn't even have to be written that cogently: mind maps, doodles, or lists of thoughts are all just fine.

CONCLUSION

Homo sapiens is the tool species. Other animals use simple tools, but ours is the only species that uses tools to make other tools. We use tools for all manner of activities, from cutting wood to cooking to documenting and remembering knowledge. To think holistically and long term, we need tools that aim to do just that. We need tools that help us plan for a better future. Remember—the aim is not delayed gratification but a new mindset that factors thinking creatively about the future into our lives today. Crucially, when tomorrow arrives—and for most of us, it usually does—it's less of a stranger and more of a familiar soul we've been visualizing along our journey.

Early in my career, the large corporation I worked for underwent a big round of layoffs. I wasn't affected, but many other people were. However, I vividly remember our VP of HR making what seemed like an odd recommendation—one I didn't fully understand at the time. She told those of us who were unaffected, "Now that you know you aren't being laid off, I recommend you go home and discuss with your spouse or significant other what you would do if you were." Why? "Because you go through that exercise with a cool head and without the pressure of dealing with the situation in real life. If you ever get laid off, you will remember how you thought you would approach it and react more rationally." My HR VP wasn't trying to alarm us or imply we all had layoffs in our immediate future. She was giving us a tool—something we might need in the future because we worked in a large organization. This tool is a classic example of one that helps you make better decisions today to benefit you tomorrow.

On a more uplifting note, both philosophers and psychologists tell us that giving is better than receiving. Research indicates the power of giving and its role in personal happiness. Study after study has shown that spending money on others or giving to charity puts a bigger smile on your face than buying things for yourself. What's so powerful about me-of-tomorrow thinking is that we are actually giving not to strangers today but to other strangers: our future selves. Those people may be hard to relate to, are probably unfamiliar, and will most likely look completely different, but they are ourselves in many future incarnations. What could be a more precious gift?

CHAPTER 2

A BALANCED LIFE

You will never find time for anything. If you want time you must make it.

—CHARLES BUXTON

Most of us spend too much time on what is urgent and not enough time on what is important.

—STEPHEN COVEY

Chapter 1 was about balancing the demands of today and tomorrow. Experts tell us that this intertemporal decision-making and prioritization is inherently tricky. It goes against the grain of both our natural inclinations and the seize-the-day messages that constantly bombard us. We need a disciplined way of thinking and new habits to master it. Sadly, failure to consider the future me causes many people to lead lives full of regret.

However, none of us can hope to perfect the art of evaluating today-versus-tomorrow decisions if we lack a set of lenses through which to view those decisions. Me-of-tomorrow decision-making has many dimensions. Chapter 1 offered a new approach and some useful mental exercises to optimize that balance between today and tomorrow. But it is also crucial to think about how you build your decision-making framework and what dimensions you need to consider.

Living a fulfilled life requires mastery of another kind of balance that's just as challenging and complicated. I'm referring to the balance among our different mes—among the different roles we play in our day-to-day lives. We become entirely different people depending on our role in any given moment: coworker, parent, friend, and so on. To achieve balance among these roles, we need to grasp some new realities and throw away many of our preconceptions. That is the subject of this chapter: a balanced life.

THE MYTH OF WORK-LIFE BALANCE

The term *work-life balance* has been in everyday use since the 1980s. If you google the term, you will get about a billion hits, almost fifty million articles, and lists of hundreds of books. By the second week of 2020, a new book on the subject had already been published! There's even a *Work/Life Balance for Dummies* book.[11] When a topic makes this storied series, it's a sure sign it's become a kitchen-table agenda item. It seems like every newspaper or business magazine has dedicated dozens of issues to the subject. Some of these are about what companies can do to help employees, while others are about what we as individuals can do to help ourselves.

Some people feel work-life balance is primarily a political question. They believe we need to address work-life imbalance through public policies that promote gender equity, more robust family-leave plans, mandated workplace flexibility, and childcare provisions. They advocate for legislation to bring the United States in line with the more progressive European countries. The Center for American Progress has cited a study that claims an astonishing 90

---

[11] Katherine Lockett and Jeni Mumford, *Work/Life Balance for Dummies* (Chichester, UK: John Wiley, 2009).

percent of working mothers and 95 percent of working fathers have work-family conflict.[12]

Whether you think the issue is personal or political, it's evident that social norms have much to do with work-life *imbalance*. Like many other issues, ingrained attitudes also need to change. But I don't believe we can look externally for a silver bullet. Ultimately, however governments and corporations change the rules of the workplace, we must take responsibility for our own balance in life. As author and marketer Nigel Marsh so eloquently put it in his 2014 TED Talk, "If you don't design your life, someone else will design it for you, and you may just not like their idea of balance!"[13]

With this amount of political and media attention, organizations at least try to listen. With an eye on retaining talent in tight labor markets, many companies address employees' concerns by trying to free work time with flexible time off and work-from-anywhere arrangements enabled by technology. Some have even adopted the newfangled idea of allowing employees to choose how much paid time off to take, with no maximum mandated. Paradoxically, studies show that this policy results in employees taking less time away from work. They fear that taking too much vacation will earn them a slacker label even if their company honors the time-off request.

This example vividly illustrates how it's much harder to change ingrained attitudes than it is to change workforce rules. Every company I've ever worked for has talked about work-life balance. It's regularly cited as the number one cause of stress. Employee survey respondents routinely rate it as the number one cause of job dissatisfaction. One team of professionals in a company I know echoed the point: in the company's annual happiness-at-work survey, *work-life balance* was the number one concern, way ahead of pay and benefits. Tellingly, there was not one single practical suggestion

---

[12] Joan C. Williams and Heather Boushey, *The Three Faces of Work-Family Conflict: The Poor, the Professionals, and the Missing*, 2010.
[13] https://www.ted.com/talks/nigel_marsh_how_to_make_work_life_balance_work.

as to how to address the problem. Of course, with some jobs, it seems impossible to find a work-life balance. Some career choices are fundamentally incompatible with being totally engaged with a young family. Whatever job you're in, whether your company is lenient or apparently disinterested when it comes to your negotiating your schedule to have a fulfilling life outside work, there are some fundamental truths that I've learned:

- Companies are not going to improve work-life balance for you. It is up to you to take control of the kind of life you want to live.
- Never put the balance of your life in the hands of a corporation. Companies are designed to get as much as possible out of you. That's not a negative judgment; it's just business logic. Employees are a factor of production, and the company needs to maximize the value it gets from them.
- We all are responsible for setting the boundaries of our lives.

The other overriding truth I've learned is that most of us are thinking about this all wrong. We view work-life balance as a way of seeking equilibrium between two separate spheres: (1) *work* and (2) everything else that we bundle into a stack called *life*. We aim for a miraculous state of equilibrium in which the demands of professional and personal life are equal.

This is unattainable. I believe it is a failure of definition. People complain about work-life balance. Companies struggle to solve this problem not because employees are overworked or companies don't care but because people don't understand the essential elements of life and how to allocate time to make themselves happy.

REDEFINING BALANCE

For years, I heard from people concerned about work-life balance. I often wrestled with that balance myself. I remember being a father of a thirteen-year-old boy and an eleven-year-old girl and realizing that I wanted desperately to spend more time with them. I was also happily married and wanted to stay that way. At the same time, I recognized how much I enjoyed my professional life and the financial rewards that were starting to come my way.

These challenges forced me to think deeply about balance. I researched and studied the topic, questioning experienced people and others in the same boat as me. I can't claim to have solved the problem, but I continue to try. The following items jumped out at me:

- Life consists of a series of forces that inevitably become unbalanced. These forces are all part of our lives, and they are all connected. We need to think less about work-life balance and more about life's different dimensions. Thinking about this helps us trade off one activity for another to get more satisfaction from everything we do.
- We need to approach balance differently. That means addressing all our needs: intellectual, physical, emotional, and spiritual.
- We should always be conscious of the implications of spending an extraordinary amount of time in one particular dimension.
- Small things matter. Think about what an ideal life looks like for you now. Your priorities today are different from what they were ten years ago and from what they will be ten or twenty years from now. We can all learn from role models, but remember: their life balance has changed over time. Steve Jobs wasn't always a workaholic. Your retired aunt didn't always spend every waking hour with her children and grandchildren. It's about your priorities now and for the future.
- We must abandon the idea that success is about material acquisition. It's simply not true that the person who dies with the most toys wins!

As I focused on balancing work and life, it soon became easier for me to think of self and family as separate concepts within what we call life. Looking at self and family, I played a game with a few friends. We brainstormed lists of activities that provided fulfillment and satisfaction to self and family simultaneously. The idea was that anything that was fulling both to self and to family was a higher-return activity than another that was for either our own or the family's fulfillment alone.

I thought about this model over the years, aiming to find activities I enjoyed not just because they made me happy but because my wife or kids genuinely enjoyed them too. For example, when I was hooked on half and full marathons, I encouraged my wife to run with me. However, her knees didn't cooperate, and we decided to let that go. But then we found another interest we were both passionate about: cooking. This became our shared activity—that combination of something we each wanted for ourselves but that we could engage in together. We loved watching cooking shows and trying out what we'd learned from them. We also developed a taste for entertaining and enjoyed sharing our recipes with friends.

I became pretty obsessed with identifying these higher-return activities—sometimes successfully, sometimes not so much. For me, time was the input or the constrained resource. As a result, I concluded that life has not two dimensions (work and life) or three dimensions (work, family, and self) but five dimensions:

- self
- work
- family
- community and friendship
- spirituality

At the time I developed this list, I was still in my marathon-running phase. This activity was clearly in the self category. This realization caused me to examine what sacrifices the race demanded of the other dimensions of my life. Running marathons taught me an important lesson about balance. To finish a marathon running—instead of walking—required several training hours every week. Completing it in fewer than five hours required more than the minimum training commitment. Achieving a time of under four hours necessitated a whole new level of commitment. I found my time was a sliding scale. The more hours I trained a week, the faster I would finish the marathon. The more hours I trained, the less time I had for something else.

This understanding forced me to decide how much time I was willing to dedicate to running marathons and which other life dimensions would need to yield their time for the sake of the race.

This exploration helped me develop what I call my *string hypothesis*. This is a simple way to look at life's domains through the metaphor of a piece of string one yard (thirty-six inches) long.

THE STRING HYPOTHESIS

Don't worry: my string hypothesis is simple. It's nothing like string theory—the theory you may or may not be familiar with from particle physics. String theory is too complex to explore here (and way beyond my understanding); still, the commonality with my hypothesis is intriguing. The originators of string theory sought a unity of ideas. They attempted to explain all of nature's forces by modeling particles and their interactions as one-dimensional objects, or strings. The goal was to unify Einstein's theories of gravity with the other forces observed in the universe. They saw it as a way of bringing together disparate theoretical frameworks. It's still being explored and developed today.

Although I can't claim anywhere near as grand an objective for my string hypothesis, I like to think of it as an attempt to unify and manage not the secrets of the universe but life's five dimensions. Instead of wrestling with theories about work life (what can employers and policy makers do?) and home life (no end of suggestions here!), these dimensions become a unified thread through which we can evaluate life balance holistically.

My string hypothesis states that excellence and fulfillment in any one of the five dimensions *always* come at the expense of one or more other dimensions. This is simply because our time is always finite—our time is a zero-sum game.

Following a model that's easy to share and understand, equate this finite amount of time with a string one yard (thirty-six inches) long. I know it sounds a bit simple, but bear with me. No matter how smart, rich, or tall a person may be, or foolish, poor, or short, we all get that same finite length of string. And we all need to decide how to divide it up.

The way we allocate the string varies according to either the phase of life we're in or simply what we think matters more in life at any time. In the case of the different phases in life, the difference is that the amount of pull each of these dimensions exerts changes as we journey through life. However, one constant idea is that activities that impact multiple dimensions provide higher satisfaction and fulfillment than activities that impact only one dimension. Before diving into this, let's first explore the five dimensions in greater depth.

1. ME @ SELF

Self is all about activities we personally enjoy. These activities give us pleasure and satisfaction aside from anything or anyone else. For me, these are photography, running, reading books, and listening to podcasts; for others, it may be watching sports on TV, cycling, playing video games, binge-watching Netflix, and so forth. This doesn't mean other people don't enjoy the same activities; it's just that our self activities float our particular boat. When we do them, we feel self-indulgent. Obviously, these same activities may provide fulfillment in other life dimensions, such as family and community and friendship, but we do them for ourselves. Perhaps your spouse enjoys the fact that you are exercising and working off your extra pounds, but you are running because you love to do it.

2. ME @ WORK

This is also easy to understand. Most people have a job that provides income and often a sense of identity and purpose. The work part of the string includes the time and energy we dedicate to our working life overall; it doesn't mean just time in the office. Traveling and commuting is also Me @ Work, although often we can leverage this time across multiple dimensions, as I used to do when listening to audiobooks back when I commuted.

3. ME @ FAMILY

The family dimension is separate from self. It represents the time and effort expended in each of our family roles, whether as a spouse; parent; child; or even grandchild, son, or nephew, for example. The essence is that this is time dedicated to a family role, whether it involves attending a sibling's wedding, babysitting a six-year-old niece, or attending a cousin's soccer game (although, in my case, this would satisfy both family and self)—or helping Mom configure her iPhone because she mistakenly deleted her favorite app.

4. ME @ COMMUNITY AND FRIENDSHIP

The community-and-friendship dimension includes everything we do with others outside our roles as parents, spouses, aunts and uncles, and forth. This could be as simple as helping friends with moving, attending a neighbor's housewarming party, or participating in a condominium association meeting. Volunteer work would also count. We could leverage this with dimension 5 if it provides spiritual fulfillment or dimension 1 if we're running the local chess club and chess is one of our self activities. Many activities and significant time can be spent in this dimension.

5. ME @ SPIRITUALITY

I created this last dimension as separate from Me @ Self because we need room to develop aside from our material needs and our pursuit of pleasure, love of family, and maintenance of friendships. Some people find this difficult to define. Others may argue they don't need this dimension. However, for most of us, it includes the time, attention, and energy we commit to our deepest core beliefs or involves our nurturing the indefinable essence of ourselves. If you believe in something or someone bigger than yourself, this dimension has its own call on your time and energy.

DIVIDING THE STRING

What is essential and often overlooked should be obvious. How we divide our time, attention, focus, and energy among these five dimensions must be determined through *conscious* decisions. Don't let autopilot take over. If we give every dimension the same importance, each area will get 7.2 inches of string. Let's talk about some examples, shown in figure 3.

1. First is Joe Career. Joe's job is one of the most important aspects of his life. Every time he meets someone else, his first question is "What do you do?" What he does defines him. He finds a way of working his responsibility area and title into any conversation. His title is in his email signature. When Joe's not working, he's at home. He makes sure his family goes to church on Sundays. Joe's string is divided among work, family, and spirituality. He has little left for self and community and friendship. He doesn't do much socially and has slowly gained a few pounds over the years.
2. Sally Self is Joe Career's cousin. She works in an individual contributor role in a large corporation, is very fit, and loves to scuba dive. She divorced a few years ago but never had

children. You will see her at the local gym every day, and she never misses a work get-together. Her last church visit was for her nephew's christening. Self takes up the longest section of her string, followed by community and friendship. She is afforded this space because her spirituality and family dimensions are almost nonexistent.
3. Dave Church is an upstanding member of the community. He is a small-business owner who got into mobile phone distribution early. He is married, has two children, and is an elder in his church. As a business owner, he manages his own schedule, so he always attends the weekly church council meetings. He participates in several of the Sunday services, and he volunteers throughout the year in many community outreach activities. His spirituality, community, and family string components are longest. Work and self are shortest.

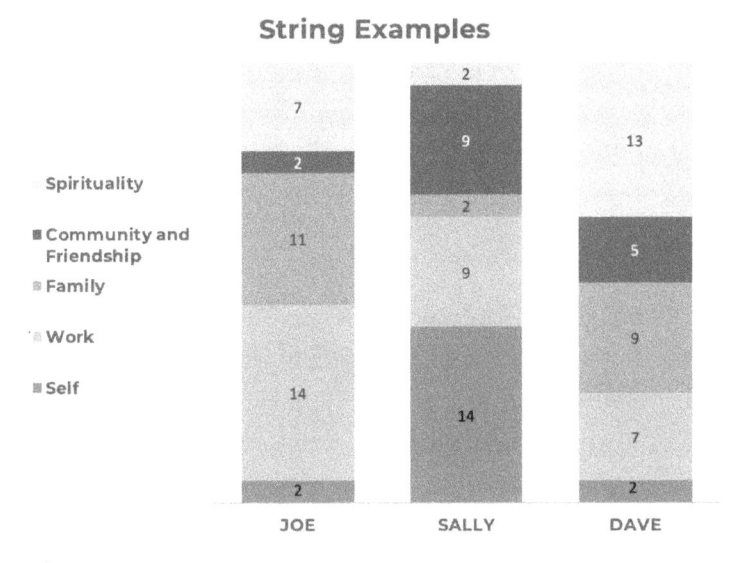

String Examples

	JOE	SALLY	DAVE
Spirituality	7	2	13
Community and Friendship	2	9	
Family	11	2	5
Work		9	9
Self	14	14	7
	2		2

Figure 3.

These simple examples show how everyone's string looks different. As a useful exercise, estimate your own using these five dimensions. Think about the components as dispassionately and honestly as you can.

It's always interesting to reflect on people you know and love and think about how their strings are divided. When I meet someone highly successful in one aspect of life, it always makes me wonder which dimension is paying for that success. Remember—nobody has more string than anyone else. Of course, some creative and high-energy people seem to squeeze more time out of each day. Still, essentially, the string is the total sum of time, energy, and focus each of us has every day of our life. While someone can be smarter or more efficient than you, the string dedicated to one dimension is a better predictor of success in that dimension than any extra intelligence or efficiency. There are always people with exceptional talent who seem to defy this rule, but ultimately, we all only get just one yard.

The string hypothesis states the following:

1. Everyone gets the same yard of string. In whatever way we try to stretch it, that's our limit, like c in Einstein's $E = mc^2$.
2. If you use the string for one dimension, it always comes at the expense of another dimension. It's always a zero-sum game. I've learned that most people don't stop and reflect on this. Just doing this exercise is an amazing and powerful act of self-discovery.

However, there is some good news. There are ways to extract more than one yard's worth of string without the string actually being longer—because it can't be. Think of it as leverage. One doesn't need to equal one or, even worse, three-quarters. One can equal one and a quarter or one and a half.

Fuzzy math, right? Let me elaborate. Everything we do doesn't need to be about only one dimension. We can choose to do things that impact more than one dimension. As a result, those activities will yield a higher return than others that impact only one dimension. For example, let's say you like to play basketball and decide to play with your friends from church. That activity impacts the self, community and friendship, and spirituality dimensions. Or you could indulge your love of golf and play with your spouse, affecting both self and family dimensions. The key is to get a double or triple benefit from a single activity.

An example from my past is my involvement in my children's swim team. I found swim meets fun, although they always start early and last a long time. Becoming the team videographer and occasional photographer then allowed me to indulge in another of my favorite hobbies. I also developed nice friendships with fellow parents. Consequently, despite those early mornings and the time commitments, these swim meets impacted the family, community and friendship, and self dimensions. It became a triple-return activity! I was there for six or seven hours, with my wife, cheering our kids. We talked with our new friends and got to take pictures and make videos, which I enjoyed immensely.

Some of you may think this is a bit crazy. By the same token, others may think people who spend all their time at work are crazy. The truth is that some people are so defined by work and enjoy it. It can do double duty as part of their self dimension. Consequently, it's a high return-on-investment activity for them.

Don't forget that everybody's self string is different: there is no right or wrong allocation of dimensions within the string. What's important is to understand the trade-offs.

UNDERSTANDING TRADE-OFFS

Of course, life is never static. Consequently, how you allocate your string will be dynamic, especially as you traverse different phases of your life. As an obvious example, your allocation will vary from when you are single to the time you are married. It will change when you become a parent for the first time or become the parent of a teenager or college student. You might expect single people to have more of their string dedicated to self, work, and community and friendship. After marriage or family partnership, you might expect the family dimension to take from community and friendship and self. Doesn't everybody gain some pounds after marriage, like Joe Career? The self part of the string becomes a lot shorter!

This tells us that to have a balanced life, we must first understand all the forces pulling us. It's much more complicated than simply work versus personal life. Understanding these dimensions helps us know how we are changing our priorities. This awareness is a powerful decision-making tool and enables us to prioritize higher-return activities: those that impact multiple dimensions. It helps us change our behavior if we are unnecessarily neglecting or elevating one dimension.

We just need to make sure that our values or desires are consistent with our actions and how we spend our time. In short, if we tell ourselves that family is important, our actions must show it. By the same token, if we realize that work is crucial to facilitate family well-being, our children's education, safety, and the like, we must pursue increasing our effectiveness at work—but not necessarily by working longer hours. I will elaborate on this in another discussion.

For me, I realized I was trading significant family time because of my travel. Although I had to travel globally, I made every effort possible to be home during weekends. The weekends I spent by myself overseas could be counted on the fingers of one hand because I looked for ways to either travel with my wife or even bring my kids on very long trips during the summer. The trade-off I made very early was never to develop habits that would take me away for hours on Saturdays or Sundays. For the same reason, I decided not to take up time-consuming self activities, such as golf and biking. This is to suggest not that we don't all need self activities—self is an essential piece of the string—but that, in my case, the travel demands of work were crowding out family.

The trade-off analysis and string allocation also come with a large caveat. There are times in life where we can't make trade-offs. Suppose we face a family emergency, such as caring for a sick relative or dealing with a physical or mental illness. In that case, we have to temporarily abandon balance and let ourselves off the hook. Nobody would suggest that allocating your thirty-six inches of string to a sick child is a poor decision.

However, we often let other events interfere with our planning. Some of these interruptions are warranted and necessary—others less so. For example, we might have a demanding boss or a financial problem that requires us to get a second or even third job. A me-of-tomorrow idea in the case of financial hardship may be to dedicate some of the string to learn a high-demand skill, such as programming or using a software tool. This is where this planning tool is incredibly useful. We all have times when planning needs to be temporarily suspended; just try not to make it a permanent condition, if you can avoid it.

In summary, to pursue a balanced life, remember you get only that yard of string. When dividing it up, think more broadly than just work-life balance. Think about what the me of a few years ahead would want. Go back to your framework from chapter 1. Is the way you are dividing the string consistent with your future me's plans?

Family and work are essential, but remember to consider activities that enrich you personally and spiritually and those that involve you in the community and nurture strong friendships. Along life's journey, your allocations will change. That's OK. What's most important is to be aware of what you're giving the highest priority to and to walk the talk. Remember that activities that impact multiple dimensions have the highest return and satisfaction. Proactively pursue those.

When you see people who are successful at work, or in any other aspect of life, first be happy for them. After that, remember such success must have come at the expense of another dimension of life. The same goes for when you see faster runners in a marathon. What are they sacrificing to train more? As the old saying goes, there's no such thing as a free lunch!

One revealing exercise is to look back at famous people and think about how their strings were divided. We tend to hero-worship people who have outstanding successes in one field. But how did that impact the balance of their lives and ultimately their fulfillment? Did they make their trade-offs consciously? Did they secretly hope for better outcomes in some of the dimensions they neglected? Or did they rationalize those achievements as being worthy of their sacrifices? As a thought experiment, here's a chart on my interpretation of the dimension allocations of historical figures (figure 4).

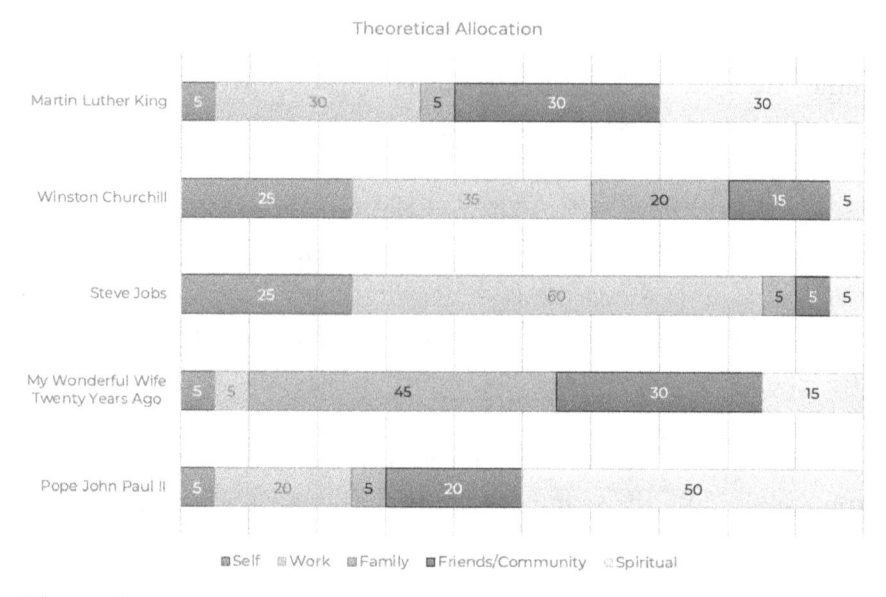

Theoretical Allocation

	Self	Work	Family	Friends/Community	Spiritual
Martin Luther King	5	30	5	30	30
Winston Churchill	25	35	20	15	5
Steve Jobs	25	60	5	5	5
My Wonderful Wife Twenty Years Ago	5	5	45	30	15
Pope John Paul II	5	20	5	20	50

Figure 4.

This is just a fun mental exercise. Historians will likely disagree. Even if these are accurate representations of their lives or certain points in their lives, there's no value judgment attached. However, it's interesting to speculate whether these are the lives they envisioned or wanted or that satisfied them. Are the allocations the result of these figures having made conscious decisions, or are they merely the result of circumstance?

PLANNING YOUR STRING

When it comes to building a balanced life, knowledge is power. The following exercise will help you develop the knowledge you need to unleash that power.

Once you've thought through the model's framework and perhaps toyed with similar thought experiments, the next logical step is to put it into practice. Understanding is nice and maybe thought provoking, but this approach's most significant benefit is the action planning you can do to help you balance your life as you want. To help you use this framework, I developed the following exercise to make the learning immediately actionable. As with much of life, it's always important to align these three elements:

1. Perception: how we think things are
2. Ideal: how we think things should be
3. Reality: how things actually are

As a challenge, I also suggest the following actions:

1. First, write down how you think your string is currently divided. How much is dedicated to self, work, family, community and friendship, and spirituality? For units of the string, you can use inches, or you can also use percentages. Write these numbers down. These will provide your perceived use of your string.

2. Next, write down how you think the string ought to be divided. This represents your ideal use of the string. I advocate being pragmatic here. The perfect division may not be entirely practical. Consider your framework from chapter 1, the phase of life you're in, the amount of time you have left to retire, the time until your children go to college, the status of your relationships, your overall economic situation, and so on. As much as we look for things to be different, there are always limits. I would argue that these limits dictate your current actions. Be aware of this reality when you plan.

Once you complete this action, the first aha should come from comparing these numbers in exercises 1 and 2, the separation of desire from reality. For extra credit, you could also address how the ideal should change in the next three or five years, depending on expected life changes.

3. The third and most valuable action has two objectives:

   a. To see what percentage of your time is dedicated to each of the five dimensions
   b. To determine how effective you are at using your time, which will help you understand the return on investment of your activities

Note that it will take a little longer, but it is crucial because this is where the rubber meets the road. This is not the perception or the ideal scenario; this is reality.

For this step, try the following exercise:

- Get a small notebook. It needs to be small enough to fit in your pocket or your purse so you can carry it everywhere. Alternatively, if you are a gadget person, use the notepad in your smartphone for this exercise and modify the subsequent steps as necessary for that medium.
- Label the first five pages of your notebook so that each page is dedicated to a different dimension: *Self*, *Work*, *Family*, *Community and Friendship*, or *Spiritual*. The goal is to take an inventory of how you use your time currently.
- Log your time. I don't advocate doing this every hour, but try at least two or three times a day. If you choose to do it three times, try noon, right before dinner, and before you go to bed. At each time, consider how much time has passed since your last entry and estimate the time consumed by each activity. For simplicity's sake, use thirty-minute or one-hour chunks. If you run out of space on a particular string (or page), go to the notebook's next page. It would be ideal to add—besides the activity and amount of time—the date, because you need to do this for a whole week. If you are

like most people, you should have 16 hours of activities per day for seven days, for 112 total hours of awake time. As you record your activities, leverage the technology available. For example, smartphones measure how much time you spend on them—log it accordingly.

Here are a few notes and examples on the third action:

- If you work forty hours a week, a disproportionate amount of time will appear in the work dimension. That's OK. Also, add in commute time (if applicable), but subtract lunchtime if you enjoy a friendly lunch with a colleague. The way I track work is the door-to-door time from morning to evening, minus lunch. That pleasant lunch goes on the community-and-friendship list. If you eat by yourself, it goes on the self list—unless you continue to work as you eat.
- Grocery shopping is family time if you do it for your family members. But it's friendship time if you are buying for a planned get-together. Think of it this way: if you weren't getting together with friends, would you be going to the store?
- When an activity includes more than one dimension, write it down on multiple pages.
- When something doesn't seem to fit neatly into a category, think of the reason you're doing it. Suppose you are ordering trophies for your daughter's softball team. Is it because you enjoy it or because you are supporting your daughter? Is it self or family?
- Let's say you spend an hour researching insurance policies. Insurance is about the well-being of our family, so it should be logged as family.
- Are you going to the hardware store to buy supplies for your yard or your pool? Count that as family time because they are for your house.

Now it's time for a few simple calculations:

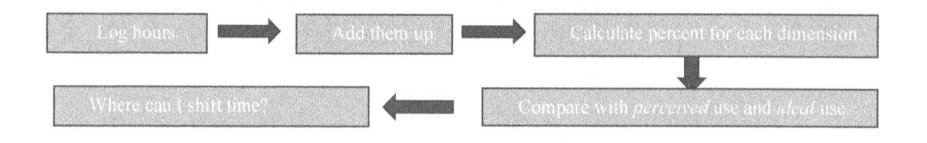

Log hours → Add them up → Calculate percent for each dimension ↓
Where can I shift time? ← Compare with *perceived* use and *ideal* use

> Maybe it is having lunch at your desk so you can get home earlier to go for a run? Perhaps it is reading a bit less every week so you can spend more time with the kids?

Remember—it's all personal, and no one will make the decision for you. You need to first want to make the changes. To calculate how effective your time is, pinpoint your awake hours:

$$168 - ((\text{number of hours asleep per night}) \times 7)$$

Most people will likely be awake for 112 hours a week. If this is your number, the activities you logged in your notebook should amount to at least 112 hours.

Now add them up. Is the sum more than your awake hours (probably 112)?

Here is the trick: hours over 112 represent time spent impacting more than one dimension.

If you don't have a surplus, don't despair. This is just the beginning. You likely have not thought about getting a high return on your time before.

Your goal should be to review the list and look for opportunities to impact multiple dimension.

If you like to walk, can you ask your spouse to go with you and make it double-return time (family and self)?

Suppose you ride your motorcycle for five hours on Saturday. Can you reduce it to three hours and look for things to do with your family or friends to turn those two hours into higher-return time? One of my friends who loved golf used to play only if his tee time was at seven o'clock or before because he wanted to be back by the time everyone was getting up for breakfast. Again, it is just about trade-offs.

The goal of this exercise is to make us reflect and align our goals with our actions. How do our strings compare to our aspirations for the different phases of our lives as outlined in chapter 1? This is an opportunity to look at the big picture. Hopefully, it will motivate you to make some changes and feel better about using your time. Even if you choose not to make changes, this practice will help you understand where you are. There is value in that. I also suggest thinking about how the strings will change over time.

CONCLUSION

Just as it's a learned habit to take account of tomorrow when making decisions today, we can learn how to balance life with some simple tools and plenty of practice. Instead of our endlessly struggling with that mythical work-life balance, I propose a framework and a system for consciously balancing our lives—that is, being deliberate about how we structure our time and priorities.

Using the framework of five essential life dimensions—self, work, family, community and friendship, and spirituality—and approaching our time, focus, and energy as finite resources represented by a yard-long piece of string, we can compare what we think our priorities are, what we would like them to be, and what our actions indicate they actually are.

Identifying these allocations will help you recalibrate your priorities. There's no right or wrong way to organize your life among these competing dimensions, but being measured and disciplined about your desires and behaviors will help you decide what to do and what not to do, as well as how to leverage high-value activities for greatest personal impact.

The string-hypothesis framework combined with the framework from chapter 1 will yield a more fulfilled me of tomorrow.

CHAPTER 3

LEARNING FOR LIFE

> All I have learned, I learned from books.
> —ABRAHAM LINCOLN

> If you haven't read hundreds of books, you are functionally illiterate, and you will be incompetent, because your personal experiences alone aren't broad enough to sustain you.
> —JIM MATTIS

Learning has no limits. Whether your topic of choice is nuclear fusion or rosebushes, filling your knowledge reservoir is life's great enabler. Think of it as building your brain of tomorrow. When you're a lifetime learner, that brain will be filled with exciting new ideas every day. You will also think more clearly and reevaluate what you learned before. It will turn you into a master of critical thinking—one of life's greatest skills.

Critical thinkers approach every one of life's challenges differently. The extra knowledge will add so many more strings to your bow and enable you to live a fuller, more successful life. As a side benefit, you'll earn more money and advance faster in your career.

Committing to lifetime learning will transform your life. As the two great Americans responsible for the chapter epigraphs pointed out, the easiest way to learn is to read. Personally, reading has helped me not only professionally; it's also provided me with instruction on how to be a better father and a better husband and even how to more thoroughly understand myself so I can improve as a human being.

But you shouldn't learn just to achieve these goals. It's not all about the end result. You'll find the process of learning, and especially learning through reading, one of life's greatest pleasures.

In fact, life itself is a full-time learning experience. Throughout history, many great people told us that seeking knowledge is the entire purpose of life—a voyage of discovery we all embark on every day of our lives.

So where did my own desire to become a lifetime learner and reader come from? I have to confess the most critical driver relates to my comment in chapter 1: my sudden realization that time is our only nonrenewable asset. I value my time and want to extract as much as I can from it. To do that, why not learn from others? Why not get to the answer faster if the solution already exists? Of course, there is value in making your own mistakes and figuring things out for yourself. But this takes time and only goes so far. I prefer to learn more things faster so I can dedicate that valuable time to other mes.

This chapter will help you appreciate the value of reading and support you on your lifetime learning journey. I'll discuss knowledge and the curiosity gene, share my personal story, and provide you with practical guidance on using the magic of reading to achieve that lifetime of learning. You will be building a brain that will enable you to make better, more thoughtful decisions. These accumulate to give you many better tomorrows.

CONGRATULATIONS! YOU'VE GRADUATED: NOW WHAT?

Cast your mind back to the day you held in your hands your very first diploma or degree—classes passed, certificate awarded, mission accomplished. Remember your feelings? Excitement, perhaps, especially if you had a job lined up or a fantastic summer adventure taking shape. Possibly trepidation about the future, especially if you didn't have a clue about your next step. But wasn't one of your feelings relief? Relief that there were no more tests to pass, books to study, or essays to write. You could go to that concert, binge-watch that TV show, or just hang out, without the stress and guilt of forfeiting precious study time.

Unfortunately, some of us take away the wrong message from that beautiful moment and the preceding years of study. We think that's where education ends. Proud of our hard-earned diplomas, confident in our expertise, we're ready to shake up the working world with our newfound knowledge. We have so much to offer: Who wouldn't want to listen to what we have to say? No more need for books or papers!

Deep down, we know that's not true. But for years, reading has dominated our lives. Books, papers, journals—always more and more to read and study, all eating into our precious leisure time and the fun business of life. Can't we have a break from all that reading?

Of course, most of us realize that we need to learn much more in any job than what we learned in school. That's universally true: even for brain surgeons and nuclear physicists, no amount of lab or classroom practice can prepare them for that first operation or self-directed experiment. For those in the business world, the gap between what we learned at school and what will make us successful is a yawning chasm. All the business training in the world, even a Harvard MBA, won't equip you to make that first executive presentation or lead that first project or team of rivals.

Even though most of us come to that realization quickly, the conclusions we draw and the actions we take are often wrong. We often narrow our focus, delve into our specialist silos, and close out much of the rest of the world that's not directly related to our work or hobbies and interests—assuming our hobbies and interests survive contact with the working world.

And after all, when it comes to our silos, can't we learn on the job, like everyone else? We'll study when we need to when it's required for the next step in our careers or—perish the thought—when we realize that we need to change careers. We think there's little point in wasting precious time learning something new until we need it—especially reading up on new ideas, when everything we need is in our pocket, thanks to the miracle of Google.

After all, isn't reading something we did back at school? This is a beguiling argument. But it's a complete fallacy. This chapter explores the benefits of lifetime learning, and it presents some simple exercises and approaches that will make you a faster, smarter, and more dedicated learner and reader. But first, I will discuss knowledge, curiosity, and why all this matters.

WHAT IS KNOWLEDGE?

So what actually is knowledge? How surprising to quote two US secretaries of defense in one chapter, as defense secretaries are rarely heroes. We usually revere the warriors who do the fighting, not those who send them on their missions. They're more likely to be villains than heroes. The late Donald Rumsfeld was no exception; he's one of the most controversial defense secretaries of modern times. At a 2002 press conference as the Iraq War was looming, he famously stated, "Reports that say that something hasn't happened are always interesting to me because as we know, there are known knowns; there are things we know we know. We also know there are known unknowns; that is to say, we know there are some things we do not know. But there are also unknown unknowns—the ones we don't know we don't know. And if one looks throughout the history of our country and other free countries, it is the latter category that tend to be the difficult ones."

At that time, debate raged across America about the presence (or otherwise) of weapons of mass destruction in Iraq. Broadly speaking, most people supported the war if these weapons existed, opposed if they did not. This quote became famous as an example of Rumsfeld's notoriously obtuse style and his penchant for muddling things. But think what you like about Rumsfeld (and this defense man will get no defense from me); this comment was insightful.

Rumsfeld's quote relates to what has become known in psychology as the Johari window (figure 5). American psychologists Joseph Luft and Harrington Ingham invented this technique in 1955 to help people improve their interpersonal relationships. People and their peers place a set of adjectives into this matrix, categorizing these personality traits as open (arena), blind (blind spot), hidden (facade), and unknown. People will then seek to grow the open square and reduce the unknown and blind squares, resulting in greater self-knowledge; disclosing the hidden square can improve intimacy and friendship.

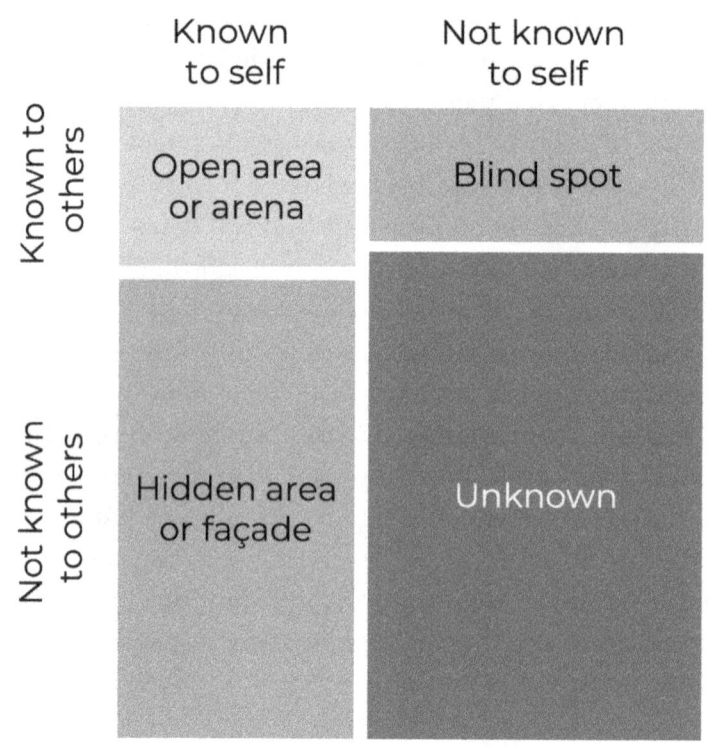

	Known to self	Not known to self
Known to others	Open area or arena	Blind spot
Not known to others	Hidden area or façade	Unknown

Figure 5.

Another way of considering these components that I find useful is through the Pie of Knowledge.[14] The team that put this idea together and first described it in the 1990s thought it looks something like this (figure 6). The pie has five slices.

---

[14] Pie of Knowledge. http://www.pieofknowledge.com/about.html.

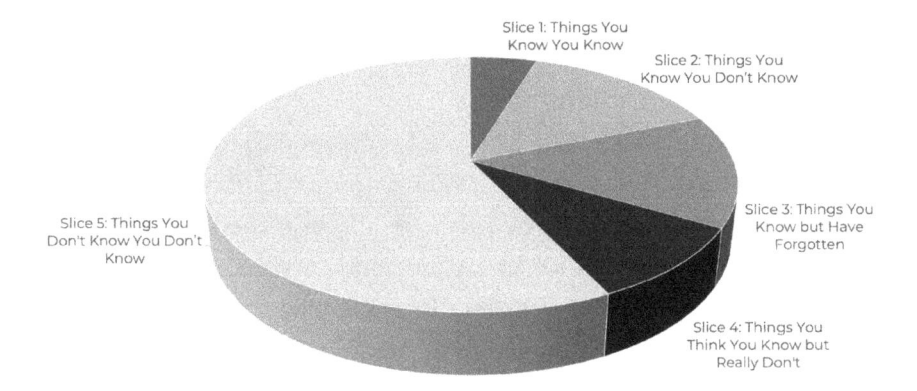

Figure 6.

- **slice 1:** things you know you know—like if I turn on the light switch, the room will become lit
- **slice 2:** stuff you know you don't know—like astronomy or solving pi to thirty-two digits
- **slice 3:** stuff you know but have forgotten—like making a great pasta sauce, or your aunt's phone number
- **slice 4:** things you think you know but really don't—like your best route to work every day or what your spouse or partner is feeling
- **slice 5:** things you don't know you don't know (unknown unknowns)—more on that later

The authors of the pie believed that understanding the four *knowing* slices—slices 1–4—helps us with lifetime learning. We should always be aiming to migrate information from slices 2, 3, and 4 to slice 1—*the things you know you know*. This is our target slice: the piece of the pie we want to grow. Much of this wisdom we can gain through lifetime learning.

As an important aside, slice 1 knowledge requires revisiting. One benefit of a lifetime-learning culture is that you train yourself to take little for granted (other than my light switch example!). This famous quote sums it up well: "It ain't what you don't know that gets you into trouble. It's what you know for sure that just ain't so."

Interestingly, almost to prove the point, most people attribute this quote to Mark Twain. However, as Quote Investigator exhaustively investigates: that ain't quite so![15]

Of course, as Rumsfeld observed, the most interesting slice is slice 5—*things you don't know you don't know*, the unknown unknowns. Objectively speaking, this slice dwarfs all the others. Probably an accurate pie chart would look completely light colored, with the other slices too microscopic to register. Leaving aside the philosophical questions of "What is knowledge?" (another fascinating topic) and "How do we actually *know* anything?" slice 5 is the unknown but exciting void of life. In fact, the thing that often trips us when we make decisions throughout our lives is forgetting how large that slice is.

For me, the pie of knowledge becomes especially useful once we've defined what kind of knowledge we're talking about. We can think about the larger pie as the universe of knowledge in our career field or particular area of expertise—for example, the marketing pie of knowledge or the financial-derivatives pie of knowledge (to choose a telling example). For sports fans like my nephew, it may be as simple as the football pie of knowledge. This knowledge is where we quickly get into a slice 5 blind spot. Many people, especially super-educated, well-read, and deeply intellectual people, get to such a level of knowledge in their field that they forget about that slice. They think all knowledge in their area is either known or at least knowable. They have a total grasp of their subject. However, slice 5 blindness can be fatal. As Rumsfeld observed, it is the slice that creates most of our difficulties.

The creators saw the pie of knowledge as a tool to help people realize their limitations, direct their education, and assist them with decision-making.

They believed it was important for individuals to migrate knowledge among slices. They point out these key challenges:

---

[15] https://quoteinvestigator.com/2018/11/18/know-trouble/.

- Know-it-alls, whose slice 4 (*things you think you know but really don't*) is too large.
- People with large slices 3s (*things you know but have forgotten*) may be suffering from deteriorating memory. With today's electronic resources, this is less of an issue: you always know where to look.
- Migrating knowledge from slice 5 (*things you don't know you don't know*) to slice 1 (*things you know you know*)? The authors think this happens randomly. If you focus on migrating knowledge from slice 2 (*things you know you don't know*), slice 5 knowledge will come through.

But is this migration random? I believe we can all accelerate this migration and change the shape of our knowledge pie. And the key to this is one of the essential traits for success in life and business. I call this the 'curiosity gene.'

THE CURIOSITY GENE

Fairly early in my career, I attended a leadership training class. I distinctly remember this as the day I discovered the truth about curiosity that got me thinking about the *curiosity gene*. The trainer discussed a large study his firm had undertaken for a big client to uncover which traits were the leading indicators of successful people in that business. The study was serious, with a large sample and rigorous statistical methods.

The results stunned me. What could matter more than the universities they'd attended, their demographic profiles, their technical expertise, and years of work experience? In those cases, the correlations were in fact weak. Overwhelmingly, the most significant leading indicators were traits like curiosity and continued learning.

Later in my career, when I was looking to recruit, I read books about which traits to look for in successful salespeople. Yet again, curiosity reared its head. The consensus was that being curious was one of the most typical characteristics. Good salespeople are always looking for the best solutions for their clients, and one way they do this is by asking a lot of questions. This explanation made perfect sense to me, and it applies to many other business roles as well. Curious people think more broadly and are more likely to develop better solutions to problems.

But is curiosity innate? Is it nurture or nature? Those of us who are parents can remember when our kids went through that phase when all they asked was "Why?" Some children take it to such an extreme that we get tired and frustrated. How many more times can a child ask "Why?" when all we're trying to do is move on to the next activity? Some kids do it out of habit, or to grab your attention, or to annoy you, or all three. However, others are deeply inquisitive, *fascinated*, taking that questioning to a whole new level that sometimes stops us in our tracks.

Children's minds are typically open to new ideas and eager to learn. They approach problems without the baggage of preconception. However, we soon know as parents that some kids are naturally more curious than others. Some almost seem to have a curiosity gene.

Obviously, I use the term *gene* in a metaphorical sense, although there seem to be naturally different degrees of curiosity. Many inquisitive children don't realize they have a gift of great value. It also occurred to me that how we respond as parents can help cultivate or hinder that unique gene. If you always have an answer at your fingertips, you shorten the inconvenient conversation.

However, there are better approaches to the fingertip answer. If we show that we don't have all the answers, we teach the child that Mom and Dad are also still learning and demonstrating curiosity, as they should. We show children that investigating the answer is interesting and worthwhile. Curiously, once my children were in college, I found myself wanting to answer their questions quickly once again. I had forgotten how important it was to encourage their curiosity. I had forgotten what it was like to be their age, wanting to learn about life. I had to teach myself to slow down and embrace their curiosity.

Just as some children are more naturally curious than others, the same applies to adults. In some people, curiosity flows through their veins. We all know people whose minds are always open to new knowledge, still researching, delving, and bringing up interesting tidbits. Other people are more matter of fact: they take life as it comes, accept a more rules-based order, and don't always question the whys of life. Some don't question life's whys but become curious when they look at their career chances.

But wherever you stand on the curiosity scale, here are three crucial facts we should all understand:

1. Curiosity is a critical attribute for success in so many areas—not only at work but also for financial and physical success. Just think about how much smarter your decisions can be if you develop an understanding of how nutrition, exercise, sleep, and savings work, for example. More on these topics later.
2. Although some people are more naturally curious, curiosity is a learned behavior. So fear not: this "gene" can be grown and developed. And I aim to show you how.
3. Curiosity is best satisfied through reading and experimenting independently, not through on-the-job training.

WHY IS CURIOSITY IMPORTANT?

Sometimes called "the father of management thinking," Peter Drucker was a huge advocate of lifelong learning. He once commented that teaching people how to learn was the most urgent task for managers. Every year, he assigned himself a topic about which he knew nothing and then made it the subject of intense study. At the core of his philosophy on strategic thinking was knowing not the answers but the right questions. He believed every business leader had to be "intelligently curious."

Many current business titans agree. In his 2015 *Harvard Business Review* article "Why Curious People Are Destined for the C-Suite," business author and innovation consultant Warren Berger quotes several CEOs on curiosity.[16] Responding to a PwC survey asking leaders to name a trait that would most help CEOs succeed, Michael Dell answered, "I would place my bet on curiosity."

Dell was not alone. Alan D. Wilson, then CEO of McCormick & Company, responded that those who "are always expanding their perspective and what they know—and have that natural curiosity—are the people that are going to be successful."

Berger's article discusses the leaders' dilemma, one I've seen played out repeatedly throughout my business career. Almost twenty years ago, I was a junior executive in a Fortune 50 enterprise facing some tough challenges. As I rose in the organization, I prided myself on fixing problems and finding solutions.

When a senior executive asked me a question, I trained myself to think, *I'd better have an answer*. If I didn't know, surely an executive would find someone who did. After all, don't executives rise through the ranks by finding solutions, not by asking questions? As former British prime minister Margaret Thatcher allegedly said about a colleague she particularly liked, "Other ministers bring me problems, but he brings me solutions."

Once, I had a manager I enormously respected. He had a sharp strategic mind and a thoughtful, cerebral manner. One day, he and I were attending a fractious meeting with some of the company's most senior executives. One leader was in a particularly belligerent mood.

The numbers were not good, and my colleague's product area was getting limited market traction. The leader needed answers. After the leader had bombarded him with questions, my colleague

---

[16] Warren Berger, "Why Curious People Are Destined for the C-Suite," *Harvard Business Review*, September 11, 2015, https://hbr.org/2015/09/why-curious-people-are-destined-for-the-c-suite.

paused, reflected, and calmly said, "I don't know, but I'm asking the team the right questions, and I'll find out."

I squirmed inside. How could you admit you don't know, don't have command of the facts, and don't have an answer at such an important meeting? But he was right. My boss was naturally curious. He was asking the right questions, doing the proper analysis, and "torturing the numbers," as we liked to say.

The lesson he taught me that day was this: you have to become comfortable with the fact that you don't know. My colleague had what Berger describes as "that rare blend of humility and confidence: humble enough to acknowledge to themselves that they didn't have all the answers, and confident enough to be able to admit that in front of everyone else." That lesson stuck with me.

TRUTH OWNERS VERSUS TRUTH SEEKERS

After years in business, I can spot the differences among executives I've led, worked with, or coached, and broadly, these people can be divided into one of two groups. My friend Miguel calls one group *truth owners* and the other *truth seekers*.

There's some of the truth owner in all of us. Maybe it's a specialist subject we learned in school or a previous job. For me, it could be salsa music or the best places to visit in Panama City. If these subjects ever come up, I can't help jumping into the conversation. My mind is yelling at me, drowning out the other person speaking. In work, this interior monologue might sound something like this: *Why is she talking about something she knows nothing about? Surely I know more about this than her—I* own *the truth. I've been doing product messaging for twenty-five years; how can that junior product manager have the audacity to lecture me? I'm the one who should be talking.*

This attitude is truth ownership, and it is a universal blind spot. Even with subjects closest to our hearts, a little humble listening might teach us something new. We should all transform ourselves from truth owners into truth seekers.

Here's what I've learned. In every facet of life, especially in business and even more so when you're a leader, there's so much more upside to being a truth seeker rather than a truth owner. Even if you think you're the smartest guy or gal in the room, be quietly curious. If you believe you own the truth, you can almost guarantee that you'll have missed a crucial nugget that another person knows and can share with you.

We don't all have the same version of the truth. There's always more to learn, maybe a slice 5 of the pie of knowledge migrating to our slice 1. Use your experience to ask great questions—seek a truth more profound than the one you started with.

Of course, truth seeking has its limits. We've all been in analysis-paralysis situations where we've tortured the numbers and done stacks of research and hours of brainstorming but still aren't happy with our collective truth. So we have to ask ourselves, "When should truth seekers stop seeking the truth?"

Everyone has a different threshold for this. Tools like the Myers-Briggs Type Indicator illustrate this; there's never an answer that satisfies everyone. I had a boss, one of the smartest people I've ever worked for. He could never quite get comfortable with the truth, as his team saw it. He'd often grudgingly acquiesce to a decision, and everyone else would leave the meeting with his approval only to discover later that he needed more research.

There's no easy answer to this dilemma. In my judgment, with most business decisions, I think 80 percent certainty works. For clinical decisions or issues of personal safety, this is obviously not good enough. In business, the critical point is where you know diminishing returns are setting in and the clock is ticking. Yes, truth seeking has to have its end point, but the crucial point is this: being a truth seeker is a universally more effective strategy than being a truth owner! So how do we seek the truth most effectively? How can we nurture that curiosity gene in all of us?

NURTURING YOUR CURIOSITY GENE

I mentioned before that some people don't see themselves as naturally curious. Maybe you weren't one of those kids continually asking "Why?" Hearing about your friend's new project or an exciting new book leaves you cold. You have work to focus on. Leisure time is to relax and unwind; after all, aren't we always told that sleep and relaxation are essential for mental health and peak workplace performance? Or perhaps you're one of those people who believes your weight of experience trumps a lifetime of other people's learning?

But think about this for a minute: Why should you have to go through life to learn things when you can pick up a book on that subject and accelerate your learning? People who don't seek knowledge are handicapping themselves, like walking in a cycling race and expecting to win.

Reading—broadly yet cleverly and selectively—using the wealth of resources at our disposal, is a crucial way of nurturing that curiosity gene. It is an exercise for the mind, just as necessary as an exercise for the body. And whether you start off curious, it nurtures that gene and makes an incredible impact on your life.

Many people still feel they are not naturally curious; however, they realize that reading is a good habit. They've come to terms with their limitations but understand the value of this practice. Naturally curious people have it easier, but even the noncurious can overcome this by coming to terms with these simple truths:

- Becoming a truth-seeking bookworm will dramatically accelerate learning.
- This added knowledge will result in achieving more *faster*.
- You will make fewer errors.
- You will be more effective.
- Decisions will be easier to make, quicker, and better.
- And, best of all, it will give you infinite pleasure.

As my story shows, the benefits accrue quickly, and curiosity is surprisingly contagious.

MY JOURNEY—SPAWNING CURIOSITY THROUGH READING

Let me take you on part of my journey. English was not my first language, and the United States was not my first country. But after years spent studying and living in the US, I wanted it to be my home. As a kid, I was reasonably smart and somewhat curious but not exceptionally so. In my twenties, the pace of life seemed fast. My main focus was on building a career and perfecting my English. I read like an average person: not obsessively and certainly not broadly.

One book that captured my imagination was Stephen Covey's best seller *The 7 Habits of Highly Effective People*.[17] But it wasn't the first six habits that spoke most to me. It was number 7: "Sharpen the saw." We always have to take time to improve ourselves, what Covey calls "unlocking the total strength, passion, capability, and spirit of each individual."

Reading is the key to improve mentally.

After a decade in my career, I rose to a position of leadership. I had managed small teams before, but this new role was different. My group was composed of people with a diverse range of talents. It included technical wizards, marketing mavens, and strategy seers. There were people with years of experience and people fresh out of college. There were people I knew and liked and people I had never met. Some worked thousands of miles away, in offices I had never visited. I was responsible for an area in which most of the team had forgotten more knowledge than I had even learned.

But this was *my* team. For whatever reason, I had been chosen to lead. I needed to inspire, provide direction, set objectives, and achieve business goals. Unlike other roles, leading couldn't mean charging forward with my machete and slashing my way through the

---

[17] Stephen R Covey, *The 7 Habits of Highly Effective People: Powerful Lessons in Personal* Change, 25th anniversary ed. (New York: Simon & Schuster, 2013).

jungle. Sitting back in my new office, contemplating this new reality with more than a little concern, I knew my objective.

More than anything else, I wanted to be the best leader I could be. I knew that the best leaders attract and keep top talent. If I learned how to attract the best talent, I would build a better team and achieve more. I knew instinctively that if that I could get the group united, supported, enabled, and even inspired, results would follow. Better still, I would have learned a skill with inestimable future benefits.

Despite what some people (often poor leaders) say, leaders are not born—they can be made. In fact, there are almost as many leadership styles as there are leaders. I had witnessed firsthand how one poor-performing sales region went from last to first with only one change: replacing the leader. I thought to myself, *A good leader can indeed make the difference.* My style would be unique but effective, transferable, and rewarding. This was the type of leader I wanted to be.

I assessed my resources. My boss was a technical genius, an engineering wizard, but not an experienced cross-functional leader. Furthermore, my experience with other bosses over the previous half dozen years had been less than inspiring. They had been more like abject lessons in what not to do rather than a template for leadership. I knew my skills and resources would only take me so far. This wasn't a role in which I could wing it.

Although short on time, I made the best decision of my career. I researched, chose, and devoured several books on leadership. I read reviews, studied authors, and plucked ideas from many fields: military leadership, political leadership, history, and psychology. I read everything I could find that I thought would help, though I can't say I read with the same level of discernment that I do today.

Some definite tips and tricks help you read more efficiently—and I'll cover these later—but for my immediate task, I was determined to get as many perspectives as possible. And it wasn't just books. I consumed every article, periodical, and blog I could find to teach me more about leadership.

My first reaction to this welter of knowledge was that putting even some of it into practice wouldn't come quickly. There was too much about nurture and support, and I cared more about effort and results at this stage of my career. Like trying on a new set of clothes, trying on these new ideas didn't come naturally. But I trusted the tailor, and I was determined to give the new suit a try.

I put one awkward recommendation to the test as quickly as possible. After the team members had gotten to know me a little, I sent them all a message asking their opinion. I provided a list of traits from my favorite book on leadership and asked them to point to me the three where I excelled, as well as those traits they hadn't observed in me. To my mind, that request itself was unconventional and also risky. How could it fill them with confidence that I knew what I was doing? However, it proved to be a turning point. My curiosity—this time about myself—became a fantastic tool for success.

Unsurprisingly, my lack of nurture came up big. One colleague told me that every other team—often teams less externally successful than ours—scheduled time to celebrate their successes, wins, and small moments of triumph. To my mind, the time taken from productive work to celebrate people doing what, after all, was their job, was alien to me. I wasn't that type of leader. I believed, above all, in tangible results.

Nevertheless, I started to create those opportunities and set aside time for those celebrations. The results were immediate. I could see changes in people's dedication and commitment. Not only did the team become more productive, but our team's reputation grew. Suddenly it became easier to attract the best new talent for open positions on the team.

It shocked me how such a little change had made such a big difference. The strengths-and-weaknesses feedback kept coming. Instead of fostering the strengths my team identified, I laser focused on those weaknesses. And I kept reading—I moved from leadership books to biographies of great leaders. I thought learning about how leaders thought about their hard decisions would help me develop frameworks for how to act in my own difficult situations.

So I had my curiosity breakthrough moment and discovered the joys of leverage, leveraging at least thirty other leaders' hard-won wisdom. But more was to come. One of the most beautiful things about reading and learning is that it's self-perpetuating. One set of ideas spawns another—the eggs spread out and become thriving tadpoles. Ideas propagate and build on each other. It was as if a whole new world of possibilities was out there.

Although I couldn't have imagined it at the time, my forced curiosity about leadership became the start of a much more impactful journey. A journey into the magic of reading was a path to becoming an obsessive truth seeker. Almost every new book or article opened up an adjacent topic that in itself demanded attention. I became fascinated as to what motivates people. My leadership compulsion led me to study behavior and behavioral economics and to better understand many of the tools of my business trade—marketing, messaging, and hence human psychology more broadly.

The fringe benefits were endless. Every new role I took piqued my curiosity, but my readings took me to ever-more-exciting places. For example, when I became a father, I wanted to develop confident children. Reading about this brought me to new ideas about building self-esteem and other parenting issues. A random *Wall Street Journal* article about fathers' role in their daughters' upbringing made me understand gender roles in parenting and life.

And so on …

THE EVIDENCE FOR READING

Everyone's story is unique. You might appreciate my journey or consider my path too demanding of time and attention. But—as I like to say in business—there is data too! While satisfying my curiosity gene, I've stumbled across many writers who cite curiosity and a love of reading and learning as essential success traits. And some bring science to the party too.

One example that struck me was Thomas Corley's *Rich Habits:*

The Daily Success Habits of Wealthy Individuals.[18] Now, I'd be among the first to say that wealth is not the be-all and end-all of success in life, but it does provide one kind of objective measure. It also correlates with success.

Corley spent five years studying the lives of rich people (defined as having an annual income of $160,000 or more and a liquid net worth of $3.2 million or more) and poor people (defined as having a yearly income of $35,000 or less and a liquid net worth of $5,000 or less). His analysis teases out what he calls "rich habits" and "poverty habits," specific behaviors associated with each group. Many patterns inevitably overlap: many wealthy people have poverty habits, and some poor people have habits we typically associate with wealth.

To me, the critical insight is the role of reading and lifetime learning.

Looking at the most influential rich habits, Corley found the following:

- Rich people don't watch TV. A full 67 percent reported "I watch TV for one hour or less per day" versus 23 percent of poor people. Only 6 percent watch reality shows, compared to 78 percent of the poor.
- As Corley explained it, "The common variable among the wealthy is how they make productive use of their time. The wealthy are not avoiding watching TV because they have some superior human discipline or willpower. They just don't think about watching much TV because they are engaged in some other habitual daily behavior—reading."[19]
- To the statement "I love reading," 86 percent of rich people agreed versus 26 percent of the poor. Rich people favor nonfiction, especially books about personal development.

---

[18] Thomas C. Corley, *Rich Habits: The Daily Success Habits of Wealthy Individuals* (Minneapolis: Langdon Street Press, 2009).

[19] Libby Kane, "9 Things Rich People Do Differently Every Day," *Entrepreneur*, July 1, 2014, https://www.entrepreneur.com/article/235228.

- Corley found that 88 percent of wealthy people read for self-improvement thirty minutes each day, compared to 2 percent of poor people.
- To the statement "I listen to audiobooks during the commute to work," 63 percent of rich people agreed versus 5 percent of the poor.

Corley described it like this: "The metaphor I like is the avalanche. These habits are like snowflakes—they build up, and then you have an avalanche of success."

Supporting data is all around us. The world's most valuable company—Amazon—is legendary for eschewing PowerPoint slides in favor of narratively written documents. This pattern, first proposed by CEO Jeff Bezos for his executive team back in 2004, has now permeated the organization.

Friends and former colleagues who work at Amazon discuss working for weeks on their papers, reading, revising, and conferring with colleagues. They spend time honing their ideas to make the best argument or tell the best story they can. Bezos wrote in a 2004 email to his team, "The reason writing a 'good' four-page memo is harder than 'writing' a 20-page PowerPoint is because the narrative structure of a good memo forces better thought and better understanding of what's more important than what." The idea is that attendees read the document before the meeting. When there's no time for that—as is sometimes the case with high-level executives—the first few minutes of the conference are spent silently reading the paper.

In his 2018 annual letter, Bezos went public on the practice and the reasons behind it. Many psychologists and neuroscientists believe that narrative storytelling is hardwired into our brains from millennia of development and survival. It's the campfire argument: stories served our ancestors as instruction, warning, and inspiration. Stories persuade because they contain emotion, the fastest pathway into our brain. Bezos is known to favor anecdotes, especially customer stories. Although his company uses "a ton of metrics" to measure success, Bezos said, "I've noticed when the anecdotes and the metrics disagree, the anecdotes are usually right. That's why it's so important to check that data with your intuition and instincts, and you need to teach that to executives and junior executives."

The ability to develop a narrative is a huge benefit curious people get from being bookworms.

BECOMING A BOOKWORM

The most common objection to reading—especially broadly and deeply—is lack of time. As we adjust to new jobs or new responsibilities in life, searching out and reading books often takes a back seat. This argument is classic me-of-today thinking. I believe the opposite is true: reading and studying *save* time. Learning from others is more efficient than learning on your own because you learn *faster*. You are sacrificing time now for massive time savings down the road. You are saving time for the me of tomorrow. It saves valuable time when you are confronted with a new topic or issue or need a new skill to navigate business and life.

Anyway, who has less free time than leaders of corporations, countries, and organizations? Jeff Bezos isn't the only successful executive who values narrative. Microsoft cofounder and leading global philanthropist Bill Gates is one of today's most prominent and influential readers. Katherine Rosman, in her 2016 *New York Times* article, notes that Gates has become a major force in publishing because of his review blog *Gates Notes*, in which he recommends books to his followers.[20] Despite his intense schedule, Gates reportedly reads a book a week. As he commented, "These days, I also get to visit interesting places, meet with scientists and watch a lot of lectures online. But reading is still the main way that I both learn new things and test my understanding."

One of Gates's most influential and wealthy friends, Warren

---

[20] Katherine Rosman, "Bill Gates on Books and Blogging," *New York Times*, January 4, 2016, https://www.nytimes.com/2016/01/04/fashion/bill-gates-gates-notes-books.html.

Buffett, himself a philanthropist and legendary investor and business leader, when asked about his keys to success, once said, "Read 500 pages every day. That's how knowledge works. It builds up, like compound interest. All of you can do it, but I guarantee not many of you will do it."

Elon Musk of Tesla and SpaceX fame once described himself, in an interview with Bloomberg, as a "bookwormy" kid. Growing up, he would read as many as two books per day. When asked how he learned how to build rockets, Musk gave a simple answer: "I read books."

Oprah Winfrey, who needs no introduction, is renowned as a voracious reader. Her book club has been running for almost two decades. She once said, "Books were my path to personal freedom. I learned to read at age three and soon discovered a whole world to conquer that went beyond our Mississippi farm."

Leaders from history often tell the same story. Winston Churchill, not a great scholar in his youth, read voraciously, especially when sent to India with the British army. His mother would send him trunk loads of books—classics, history, philosophy—from which he gleaned the keys to rhetoric and language. He became one of the twentieth century's most prolific writers and speechmakers, as well as Britain's legendary wartime prime minister. His onetime nemesis Mahatma Gandhi, father of Indian independence, also read exhaustively. His library and interests stretched far and wide, from Western philosophy and religious texts to books on science, theology, law, literature, history, and sociology.

Reading broadly and deeply is the key to success. Even for an initially uncurious mind, there are many ways to grow that curiosity gene and become a bookworm. Here are some of my favorite practical tips.

PRACTICAL READING TIPS

If you're starting to become a bookworm, you'll find plenty of internet advice on how best to organize your time. If you already have a well-honed curiosity gene and read like a business leader, you probably have your method. However, as a well-traveled book addict who has read through many churns of the technology wheel, I want to offer my five most important tips.

1. CHOOSE YOUR BOOKS CAREFULLY

Most of the time, like in my leadership story, you'll know your target topic. You'll be confronted with a challenge that requires a specific set of skills or a body of knowledge. Of course, in every area, there are so many choices of books. Reviews on Amazon, while useful, are only part of the answer.

First, you should ask other people: colleagues, friends, neighbors, those you know who've probably been in the same boat, or those whose professional opinion you value. What books particularly spoke to them on this topic, and why? If the books they recommend don't work for you, you'll soon find out.

If your reading isn't related to a specific challenge and you're just sharpening the saw (which we should all do), use lists. The ones I reference include *New York Times* best sellers, recommendations from celebrities like Bill Gates, and even bathroom books. If you have never heard of this last type of book, you should look into them. I discovered Covey's *7 Habits* on a bathroom book list.

I believe there's value in reading fiction now and again, especially if you weren't exposed to much literature at school. There are so many classics that are easy to read and make us think about everyday things differently.

2. FIND THE FORMAT THAT WORKS BEST FOR YOU

There are three basic book formats: (1) physical copy, (2) electronic book, and (3) audiobook. Even with older volumes, there is an increasing availability of all three forms, although sometimes you have no choice.

I can't emphasize enough that there's no right answer as to which format is best. I think it partly depends on your individual learning style. Sometimes you have to try a few methods and see which suits you best.

Psychologists endlessly debate whether reading or listening is better for comprehension and retention, with the academic bias typically toward active reading rather than passive listening. In his 2018 *New York Times* article, against the background of rapidly accelerating audiobook and flat print and e-book sales, Daniel Willingham evaluated the state of the evidence as to which format is better for learning.[21]

His short answer is *it depends*. He found that for difficult texts, reading is usually more effective; for simpler narratives, there is little difference. Physical reading is also faster. In his recent meta-analysis of 190 studies across multiple countries that use the Latin alphabet, Belgian psychologist Marc Brysbaert found that adults' average reading rate was 238 words per minute—significantly lower than the oft-quoted 300. Professors and academics often read twice as fast. However, even the average person's reading rate easily beats audiobook listening, which comes in at about 150–160 words a minute.

Therefore, from the perspective of comprehension, there's little objective difference between the written and spoken word. Bill Gates carries around a suitcase full of books—his medium is print. But with

---

[21] Daniel Willingham, "Is Listening to a Book the Same Thing as Reading It?," *New York Times*, December 8, 2018, https://www.nytimes.com/2018/12/08/opinion/sunday/audiobooks-reading-cheating-listening.html.

all due respect to one of the most tremendous present-day examples of learning through reading, my approach is different.

Although I know listening is slower than reading, the spoken word has the crucial advantage of leverage. I'm a legendary multitasker and, as I explained in the last chapter, someone who likes to have a high return on investment with his activities. I almost always start by buying books in audio format. I listen while I'm driving, jogging, walking, or doing any activity that's more or less automatic. Sometimes I'll stop my impulsive multitasking and take notes. And I nearly always increase the standard reading speed in my app, just a tad. People sometimes ask me how I read so many books. I tell them, "I don't read books; I listen to books!"

At any one time, I probably have one hundred audible books accessible. I crank through them. If I find one compelling, or if the book has charts, diagrams, and frameworks that I think I'll need to reference, then I buy the e-book edition. I keep my top twenty go-to reference books on my e-reader at all times—ready to jump in and read or reference whenever spare time allows.

If it's a book that I value highly—a lifelong reference that I want to show people at home—then I'll purchase a third copy, in the physical format. While it may feel wasteful, both in terms of money and the earth, to own a book in multiple formats, I find the flexibility useful.

But I would emphasize that these habits are unique to me. Note, too, that libraries are making a comeback, and there are electronic lending services. It's been noted that millennials are more likely to use libraries than baby boomers and those of Generation X. You do have to find your own rhythm and process, as long as you commit to the goal of reading for lifelong learning.

3. MANAGE YOUR TIME

You may have learned or read about so-called academic reading techniques, especially speed-reading. Depending on which expert you ask, there are anywhere from three to seven different methods. If you can speed-read effectively, great, but I think it's more important to develop your reading *skills* than your reading *speed*. Being focused and selective in your reading habits will reduce your time spent reading and make you more effective.

Some people believe good reading is best accomplished in large blocks of time. There's no doubt that uninterrupted chunks give you the greatest scope for focus and careful thought—an ideal way to absorb and learn. Some experts believe you should always set a timer, whether you have thirty minutes or three hours, allowing you to devote the entire time, free of interruptions, to reading. The idea is that committing helps boost productivity.

To me, reading has a rhythm. You'll know when the mind needs to move on, but only after you've given your reading an intense turn. And, as I mention before, I absorb myself in learning through listening. You can turn on and off at the click of a handset.

But don't be impractical, and definitely don't ignore spare moments. Those fifteen minutes before an appointment or half hour on the subway may seem suboptimal, but even if one or two key thoughts surface, they were well worth the time. As long as you get back to the book quickly, the ideas you gained in those fleeting moments will stay with you.

Some research shows that you absorb more information right before bed, and reading helps you sleep better. Besides, reading at that same time every day makes it easier to form a consistent routine. Whether that's the best time of day varies from person to person. Pay attention to your best times of day, but whatever you choose, never relegate your reading to your day's margins, when you're more tired.

The most important advice I received was this: never get caught out without reading material. I learned this from one of my senior managers. A recent autobiography of a former US president stresses the same point. Always have something to read (or listen to) in case a meeting starts late or an appointment is unexpectedly canceled. There's nothing more frustrating than wasting that precious block of time that you've just been gifted.

4. UNDERSTAND THE VALUE OF ADJACENCY

I'm just about old enough to recollect the early days of the World Wide Web. One of the novel joys was that splendid innovation—*hyperlinks*. Suppose you had a decent-enough internet connection (which was rare). In that case, you could spend time following one thought or subject to another. The idea of linked documents was a novel approach that we all now take for granted. Hyperlinks from one page to another are less useful than just narrowing a search and following threads that way.

I tend to think of reading a little like useful hyperlinks. If you're focusing on a topic, don't be afraid to look for exciting adjacencies. Particularly in the field of personal development or in areas like leadership and marketing, there's plenty of topic overlap. A book may be titled something off topic from your central mission but contain valuable content. Also, the detour could lead you into another educational area altogether. What fun would that be? Once you start reading on a topic and find out you like it, don't necessarily switch. Look for related things. That journey took me from leadership to human understanding to psychology. That was a profoundly enriching journey.

5. WEIGH YOUR BOOK

Of course, I don't mean literally. But successful readers are selective about their content. Whether you're choosing from several book options on a subject or you're considering a book that comes highly recommended, effective reading requires a smart, maybe ruthless, approach.

To start with, I rarely buy an audiobook more than ten hours long, unless it's a masterpiece—that is, unless the reviews are spectacular and it's something I absolutely must read.

First, I like to step back and think about what I want to get out of the book. Am I searching for something specific? Do I want a broad overview, or is this an instruction manual with detailed knowledge I wish to acquire?

Then, I survey the text: I read the preface, introduction, contents, summaries, and conclusions (unless it's a biography or fiction, as that would spoil the narrative). I see from this which chapters I'll need to dig into deeply and which could do with more cursory treatment.

Get a book you can handle. I usually give each book three chapters to prove its worth. After weighing the book, decide if the book needs to be skimmed or deeply absorbed. If you plan to skim, focus on the book's introduction and conclusion, the first and last paragraph in each chapter, and the first sentence in each paragraph. To absorb, I'm much more thorough, but if I find the author excessively repeating the same point in slightly different ways, I'm quick to move on. My advice is to stay alert and flexible as you read. Your technique will develop quickly.

EXERCISING YOUR CURIOSITY GENE

If you are new to systematic reading and exploring topics in detail, starting might seem daunting. As I mentioned, I was not an exceptionally curious kid—just average, like many people. At first, like with the student graduating from college thrilled at having no more papers due, dedicating time to building reading lists and researching subjects seemed difficult. It wasn't something I could imagine doing every time I faced a new challenge.

However, the remarkable thing about immersing yourself in new topics is that it pulls you in and gets so much easier every time. I have found it a deeply fulfilling way to work through new ideas and form judgments. I believe that one of the crises of modern discourse in our information-saturated world is that complex subjects often get reduced to a headline, a tweet, or a widely circulated meme. Don't mistake information breadth for depth. Only by digging deep and using critical thinking can you readily distinguish facts from disinformation.

If you are keen to try my recommendations but new to topic immersion, I suggest the following:

1. **Pick a topic.** Maybe, like my earlier example about leadership, the topic relates to a new challenge you're facing at work or a new skill that can enhance your career. Or it could be a subject like investment strategy, health maintenance, or relationship improvement—any of the issues I address in subsequent chapters. Make sure your topic is broad enough to encompass different opinions but narrow enough to give focus to your reading.
2. **Examine lists, recommendations, and reviews.** You can use the lists I discussed earlier on or seek guidance from people whose opinions you value. If your topic is controversial, make sure you select books offering different ideas or points of view.
3. **Purchase books in your preferred format.** If you suspect you are primarily an auditory learner, like me, purchase a few audiobooks. However, remember this format is more time consuming and ideal for multitaskers, perfect for listening while exercising or commuting. If you are unsure, try different books in different formats and see which works best for you.
4. **Set a reading goal, and communicate it to friends and family.** To start with, set a modest target of a book per month. As you get into the flow, you can increase this. Once you have decided on your target, share it with selected friends and family—people you communicate with regularly. In this way, they can hold you to account periodically, and you will enjoy telling them of your progress and your success.
5. **Recommend books to others.** When you've completed steps 1–4, get into the habit of recommending books to other people with similar interests. It's a wonderful way of sharing the magic of learning, and it often leads to great idea exchanges and new topics to explore.

CONCLUSION

In your entire life, you'll only scratch the surface of entire human knowledge. You may never expand your slice 1 of the total pie of knowledge (*what you know you know*) enough to make much of an impact in shrinking slice 5 (*what you don't know you don't know*).

But the evidence shows, and my experiences have taught me, that the impact of the effort is monumental in terms of your achievement and happiness. Paradoxically, becoming a reader will also save you time. You will learn more and learn it faster.

Of course, fast learning has many other benefits, not least your life balance, discussed in chapter 2. Focused learning will leave more of your precious time available for different dimensions of your string, enabling you to be more effective at work, at home, and in your community. Learning also helps you take care of that most important me, in whose absence there are no other mes: the Me @ Me. When you develop the curiosity gene and nurture it with a dedication to learning through reading, life becomes immeasurably richer in every way—more interesting, more exciting, and happier. That is my continual journey and lifetime habit, and like any habit, it can survive the stress test of life.

Most recently, as I have tried to nurture my curiosity gene, I have also added podcasts to my portfolio of truth-seeking tools. What's fascinating is that many of my favorite podcasts have led me to books because they often involve interviews with authors on a topic of interest to me. As such, I have started using podcasts as a way to find great new books.

Finally, the most beautiful thing about knowledge is that it helps us better frame our future mes. It shows us more clearly what's possible and also how to get there faster.

CHAPTER 4
RELATIONSHIPS OF TOMORROW

> If civilization is to survive, we must cultivate the science of human relationships—the ability of all peoples, of all kinds, to live together, in the same world at peace.
>
> —FRANKLIN D. ROOSEVELT

So far, this book has been all about you—or should I say *me*? The me of tomorrow, the five mes, and the better me (i.e., me as the lifetime learner). You may have noticed something missing: other people. In fact, how can you plan for the me of tomorrow at age thirty, forty, or fifty if the Me @ Community and Friendship or the Me @ Family doesn't involve good relationships with other people? Without them, focusing on the benefits of the me of tomorrow is pointless. Relationships are the substance of life; they nourish us, support us, and define us. Relationships are also our legacies: the intangible effects on others that endure during our lives and after. Legacies are how we change the world.

MISSING PEOPLE

As I wrote this chapter during the painful pandemic months of 2020, other people were missing—literally. There was a coronavirus lockdown affecting more than half the world. If you look back years from now at your 2020 social media feed, you will undoubtedly recognize a stark illumination of the psychological strain of the time.

Later in 2020, many commentators were busy consigning the year to the trash can of memory. Some called it the worst year ever. There were no friends; coworkers; extended family members; or even other people to meet in restaurants, clubs, and cafés. It took no crystal ball to tell us that the rates of depression and even suicide would sadly increase during this period.

The relationships we have with other people lie at the heart of life, and evidence suggests that we need them more than ever. As the old Turkish proverb says, "No road is long with good company." The 1960s song for the musical *Funny Girl* put it another way: "People who need people are the luckiest people in the world." If we think we don't need people, we are genuinely unlucky. Whether for love, companionship, self-validation, a spark of creativity, problem-solving, or any manner of things, relationships are as vital as the air we breathe.

THE UNIVERSAL PROBLEM

Of course, the vital importance of relationships is not remotely controversial, although some cultures highly value self-reliance and independence. These cultures tell us we must be strong, independent, and self-sufficient. By all means, we need reservoirs of self-motivation and personal autonomy. But that doesn't mean that we can avoid being good at personal relationships. Not only are these nourishing and fulfilling in themselves, but they are also essential for success in business and in life.

As Roosevelt described it, ignoring the "science of human

relationships" hurts us in many ways. Throughout my years of business coaching and counseling, the most common problems people have asked me about involve their relationships, whether with bosses, coworkers, customers, or teams.

At one time or another, we have all struggled with relationships. When you analyze problems in peoples' working lives, a majority of these problems are relationship related:

- a salesperson struggling to close deals
- a production manager wrestling with declining productivity
- a product manager unable to deliver on schedule or budget
- a school administrator losing staff

Sometimes these salespeople, product managers, or administrators lack skills, experience, training, and self-discipline. However, in the overwhelming majority of cases, these deficiencies are not the root of the problem. Nine times out of ten, the root cause is the failure of a human relationship. Again, you most likely agree with this. But what do we mean by a *relationship problem*? After all, what is a relationship?

If you think a relationship is just about two people's interactions and their ability to communicate effectively, that's only half the story. Could it also be the fulfillment of desire, a sense of belonging, a transaction, a series of moments in time, an opportunity to express one's opinions, a shoulder to cry on, or a chance to get advice for the future?

In reality, a relationship can be all these things. Uniquely, it's also a state of mind—an indefinable, unspoken, amorphous idea, or a mental image, opposite another embodiment in the other person's mind. Simply put, your brain creates that image, and a relationship problem is with that image. It's often how you define it; what expectations come along with it; and how it conflicts with the idea your spouse, friend, child, or coworker holds him- or herself.

People struggle with the most intimate personal relationships just as much as the most superficial relationships. In fact, fewer of us are engaging in that closest of all relationships in the US:

marriage or life partnership. According to a survey from the National Opinion Research Center at the University of Chicago, 35 percent of respondents reported having "no steady life partner" in 2018, up from 28 percent in 1986—an extraordinary increase in only one generation.[22] Among people aged eighteen to thirty-four, the number has ballooned from 35 percent to 51 percent over the same period.

Obviously, marriage is not the only partner relationship, but marriage statistics can be a useful proxy for partnerships overall. In a 2017 report from the Pew Research Center, most unmarried people said they were not married because they just hadn't found "the right person."

People struggle, especially with the most intimate relationship of all. If we are to look holistically at the me of tomorrow, we need to think about our relationships of tomorrow. No amount of future-seeking, life-balancing, knowledge-enhancing effort will make us more successful if we don't address the elephant in every room: human relationships.

FRAMEWORKS

You may have noticed by now that I have a business mindset and I love frameworks. However, because human relationships are intrinsically complex, building frameworks to solve relationship problems is exceptionally challenging. This chapter addresses relationships head-on and helps you think about them as clearly and dispassionately as possible. I lay out my golden relationship rules and examine some particular types: spouse or partner, siblings, children, friends, and colleagues. I provide tips on managing those tricky work relationships that trip us up and hinder our career progress.

Much of my advice is about attitude: how you view a relationship in your mind. However, I offer some practical tips too—tips I've

---

[22] NORC at the University of Chicago, "Trends," https://gssdataexplorer.norc.org/trends/Gender%20&%20Marriage?measure=posslq.

found useful in tuning up that relationship gene and making you the best you can be. But first, you may ask, why does any of this matter? Why do I need to work at improving my relationships?

WHY DOES THIS MATTER?

People consistently underestimate the value of good relationships. However, an increasing body of evidence suggests that people with enjoyable, productive, and close personal relationships live longer, happier lives.

In his famous 2005 cover story for *National Geographic*, American author Dan Buettner identified "Blue Zones"—places across the globe where people live longer, happier lives.[23] Initially, he identified three such areas: (1) villages in the Barbagia highlands of the Italian island of Sardinia; (2) the Japanese island Okinawa; (3) and some Seventh-Day Adventist communities in Loma Linda, California. He has since added other places to the list.

Buettner analyzes the habits and lifestyles of people in these regions. He tries to understand what makes them different from the rest of the human tribe.

Physical elements like diet and exercise are essential—after all, longevity is a physical phenomenon—but focusing only on the physical buries the lead. When Buettner concluded his 2005 TED Talk (which is well worth a listen), he identified the most compelling finding from all his research: the foundation of longevity in these clusters is how the people there *connect and relate to others within their community*.

Their network of relationships is stronger than those most of us have. The example from Okinawa illustrates this dramatically. People meet regularly with close friends they've traveled through life with, a concept they call *moai*. Buettner showcases a group of ladies who've been together for more than seventy-five years. He concludes, "Your friends are long-term adventures and therefore, perhaps the most

---

[23] Blue Zones, "Biography," https://www.bluezones.com/dan-buettner/.

significant thing you can do to add more years to your life and life to your years." Buettner tells us that those good relationships are the key to longevity.

But living a long life is one thing, living a happy one another. Studies like those of Blue Zones focus on life's length, but there's also a stack of independent evidence of how relationships make us happier. In fact, positive relationships—not just intimate life partnerships but all our relationships across life's spectrum—are *the* most critical determinant of overall life happiness and satisfaction.

We *Homo sapiens* are the most social species of all mammals. Humans have an innate and compelling need to form and maintain strong interpersonal relationships. Volumes of research argue that positive social connections make us happier. Relationships connect to our most powerful emotions. And positive ones project happiness, contentment, and calm, whereas negative ones project anxiety, depression, and loneliness.

I found one of the most compelling pieces of evidence as to why we could care in the Harvard Study of Adult Development, a research project that began more than eighty years ago. The project didn't start out trying to measure human happiness but has morphed into one of the most fascinating and longest-running measures of precisely that.[24] It's quite possibly the most extended study of its kind ever undertaken. The original researchers selected 724 men: some were Harvard sophomores, and others came from deprived areas of inner-city Boston. Future president John F. Kennedy was one of the original participants.

Through regular, consistent contact with the subjects, the researchers tracked every aspect of their subjects' lives, using multiple methods, including questionnaires, medical data, and even brain scans. As the original participants aged and died off, the study was expanded into the second generation.

As you can imagine, the data output from such an extensive study is voluminous. The research covers hundreds of factors: physical,

---

[24] Harvard Medical School, https://www.adultdevelopmentstudy.org/.

mental, financial, career, and fame. Fame and fortune are factors that many millennials have identified in recent American surveys as keys to a "good life."

Some of the research participants have done well (one even became president); others have consistently struggled throughout their lives. However, when you take account of every factor in the study, one central lesson emerges. In his 2015 TED Talk (also well worth watching), current study director Dr. Robert Waldinger delivered an unequivocal message: "The lessons aren't about wealth or fame or working harder and harder. The clearest message we get is this: good relationships keep us happier and healthier." He went on to cite three key learnings:

1. Social connections are good, and loneliness is toxic, a silent killer that one in five Americans suffer from today.
2. It is not the number but the quality of our relationships that makes us happier. When you reach age fifty, the biggest determinant of whether you'll live to eighty is whether you're satisfied with the quality of your closest relationships.
3. Good relationships protect and nurture our brains. People who have the kinds of relationships where they can really count on people—relationships of mutual care and protection—have sharper memories and more active minds as they age.

These findings are compelling. Other physical or psychological studies reach the same conclusion. They show that when people feel lonelier, they have higher levels of the stress hormone cortisol, which raises the risk of heart disease and creates other health problems.

Emiliana Simon-Thomas, science director of the Greater Good Science Center at the University of California, tells us that the lack of a social support system causes chronic physiological stress.[25]

When you think about it, it doesn't take a Harvard study or an ethnographic analysis of Okinawan centenarians to tell us what we

---

[25] https://ggsc.berkeley.edu/?_ga=2.36627680.1368640904.1599050094-1790775514.1599050094.

know to be true. Rich and conventionally successful people, even those who achieve the fame and fortune that many young people consider the essential ingredients of a happy life, are not especially happy.

During my career, I've seen many smart and "successful" business leaders fail at what these studies tell us are the keys to a long, happy, and healthy life: sustaining relationships. They have failed in achieving this in many of life's domains, most noticeably close personal ones.

A group of people who exemplify staggering success—Hollywood celebrities—have a divorce rate of 52 percent, more than twice the US population's level, as measured in the 2017 census. World leaders who achieve the pinnacle of political life often fail in similar ways. This has been demonstrated spectacularly by several US presidents: men who struggled with intimate relationships, had angry and unstable relationships with advisers and colleagues, and suffered from deep personal unhappiness. Clearly, acquiring fame and fortune does not equal success in the most crucial determinant of human happiness: the quality of your relationships.

MY RELATIONSHIP RULES

By now, I should have convinced you that relationships matter. Developing and maintaining high-quality relationships is crucial for your health and happiness.

Of course, not all relationships are equal in their impact on our lives. How you build strong, meaningful connections will differ dramatically according to whether they're with life partners, siblings, children, friends, and business associates. Later, I'll drill a little deeper into some of these categories. However, first, I'll share some universal rules that apply to every life relationship. Think of them as the baseline: the minimum requirement to develop and sustain human relationships. I'll then layer on some specifics and provide exercises to give all your relationships a tune-up.

RULE 1: UNDERSTAND YOURSELF

This might sound counterintuitive. After all, don't we improve a relationship by better understanding the other person? However, self-discovery is absolutely vital to this process. If relationships are, to some degree, mental images, then matching these images with others has to start with ourselves.

Understanding ourselves sensitizes us to the wide variety of personality types around us. It makes us aware of how our personalities can conflict or harmonize with other people's. It helps spark that flash of intuition as to why we are having such trouble collaborating with a particular coworker or solving a specific issue. So knowing how your image may be different from another's helps you adjust your approach and communication style to become more productive and effective.

Patterns of human behavior have been sliced and diced by psychologists for decades. Every business I've known has used some kind of employee personality assessment. They use these assessments to understand how people might work together, build teams, minimize or at least explain conflicts, and match different personalities with partners and customers.

I love these tests because they remove judgment and allow you to simply think. Often there's no right or wrong answer but rather different ways to approach problems or lenses through which to view life. I have done enough of these assessments not to recommend one over another too strongly. I have seen them all either used effectively or discarded rapidly by organizations. Armies of consultants and reams of literature and corporate development tool kits support each method. Here, I will refer to three with the greatest longevity.

1. **The Myers-Briggs Type Indicator, or MBTI,** based on work by Katherine Briggs and her daughter Isabel Myers more than forty years ago. Grounded in Jungian psychology, it has been used by millions of people. It focuses on the following four key personality dimensions:

1. Favorite world (extraversion or introversion)
2. Information (sensing or intuition)
3. Decisions (thinking or feeling)
4. Structure (judging or perceiving)

MBTI scores people on these criteria, creating sixteen personality types.[26] People know them by their initials: ESTJ, ENTJ, INFP, and so forth. Its value in organizations is well documented. There are companies where MBTI scoring is so embedded that people attach their personality types to their internal email signatures. It tells their colleagues, "I know myself, and remember this when you are working with me."

2. **The DISC assessment**, based on the work of early twentieth-century psychologist William Moulton Marston.[27] Like Myers-Briggs, DISC uses four dimensions:

   1. Dominance
   2. Influence
   3. Steadiness
   4. Compliance

DISC measures the strength of each of these tendencies and maps people to style cards based on the extent to which they trend toward them.

3. **The Enneagram** is more complicated and consequently has many professional psychological adherents. This model creates nine personality types and assigns a person into one category, with nuances that show tendencies and connections to other categories. Many Enneagram adherents take it beyond workplace use and apply it to issues of spirituality and personal development.

---

[26] https://www.myersbriggs.org/my-mbti-personality-type/mbti-basics/home.htm?bhcp=1.
[27] https://www.discusonline.com/disc/what-is-disc.php.

Some corporate HR departments get quite religious about their preferred approach to these popular personality typologies. A partner company of mine swore by the DISC method—everyone proudly claiming allegiance to "team red" or "team blue." Others swear by MBTI—that's certainly the one I've used most often in my journeys in corporate America. There's an ever-expanding human-development industry lying behind each of these approaches.

Having become quite familiar with these three assessments—as well as a few others, like Gallup's CliftonStrengths, which I have also found useful—I have a slightly more nuanced take on their effectiveness and use.[28] I'm a framework person. I support dispassionate, unemotional, almost academic approaches to situations. It helps me understand them better. But I'm wedded neither to any particular one of these methods nor to others that become fashionable among psychologists and human behavior theorists now and again. As a believer in human development, I see that these tests and their diagnoses are essential tools. None of these on its own is a universal human development tool kit; humans are much too complicated for that. But if your organization offers you any of these programs (other than the free online tests that seem to leave more questions than answers), embrace it enthusiastically.

The act of taking these tests alone is therapeutic. It makes you think deeply about your attitudes, behaviors, and habits. While incomplete as a measure of your whole personality, the diagnosis will help you build your understanding of yourself. Take what is useful from the process; none of it will be wasted. It will provide signposts on that lifelong journey of self-discovery we should all be taking.

There's another vital thread too. When we take these tests and compare our results with other people's, it dilutes the personality judgment we may have made through some problematic interactions. It leaves less room for personal animosity. The issues we are having become less personal. It helps us see less *right and wrong* and more about the difference. It gives us a new lens through which to understand the

---

[28] https://www.gallup.com/access/239204/cliftonstrengths-assessment.aspx

challenges we may have, which takes away from our natural tendency to be judgmental. In fact, if I could add one subrule to understanding yourself, it would be to stop yourself as soon as you start judging.

The Myers-Briggs Type Indicator has helped me in my personal life and my business life. One big aha in my relationship with my wife came soon after she also took the MBTI test. Her decision-making is so firmly based on feeling—180 degrees from mine, which is based on thinking. This insight has been invaluable when we come to different conclusions on a decision. I know I'm a thinker, but I now realize that my way is not the only way. Making decisions based on feeling, like my wife does, is different but just as valid. My decision-making process considers my feelings less than hers. This understanding has saved me some useless fights with my wife. We both know that we approach decision-making from different places.

An example of how knowing other people's MBTI scores is so useful comes from my immediate family. Last year, we sat down to plan our family vacation. The conversation was long. Most of the family wanted to explore all the options. I listened for a short time and quickly came to the conclusion that they were overthinking it. I had already made up my mind. I wanted to make a decision and go.

Simply, in terms of structure—organizing one's life and environment—most of my family members lean toward perceiving rather than judging. Perceivers organize their thoughts differently. They take longer to make some decisions. I am wired differently. I lean toward judging. I like to make decisions faster. Being diametrically opposed to my wife on the decision-making axis (thinking versus feeling) made the conversation even more complicated.

Before I understood my family and where everyone stood in the MBTI framework, there would have been a world of conflict and frustration. However, because I understood this framework and the differences between us, I was surprisingly calm and patient during the family vacation discussion.

I have run into the same issues many times in my working career, but having this framework is incredibly helpful. As soon as I feel frustrated or start labeling people, I fall back on that framework. Just understanding where the other person is in the framework compared to yourself is incredibly empowering.

RULE 2: ABANDON YOUR ARBITRARY PRECONCEPTIONS

In chapter 3, I discussed the Johari window and the pie of knowledge. I referenced the infamous Donald Rumsfeld quote describing those unknown unknowns. That's the category of knowledge with which we have the most difficulty. It's a fundamental human failing to ignore or forget the vast ocean of things we don't know we don't know. That knowledge-pie slice is so much bigger than the other pieces: what you know you know, what you know you don't know, things you have forgotten, and the things you think you know but don't.

This same blind spot hurts us continually with relationships. Often, we don't know what we don't know about the other person in the relationship. As we fumble around in relationship darkness, we place arbitrary preconceptions on the relationship (our mental image) and the other person. We have a picture of what the relationship should mean, what the relationship should be like, and what's in the other person's mind.

In his best-selling book *The Subtle Art of Not Giving a F*ck*, author Mark Manson describes one such arbitrary preconception.[29]

With apologies to Mark—I'm not quoting directly—the story goes something like this. A man who frequently called his brother confessed to a friend, "I hate my brother." He'd suddenly realized that he was the one who always made the running, made an effort, initiated the call. His brother's apparent lack of interest and initiative in nurturing their relationship had made him angry and resentful. He decided that his brother was the bad guy, and his frustration boiled over.

This man was making one of the most straightforward, most

---

[29] Mark Manson, *The Subtle Art of Not Giving a F*ck: A Counterintuitive Approach to Living a Good Life* (New York: HarperOne, 2016).

common, and least recognized relationship mistakes: he had an arbitrary preconceived idea of what friendship—or, in this case, siblingship—means. Calling the other party frequently, showing interest, initiating conversation, and asking about that person's life was his idea—his mental image—of what a relationship means. Indeed, isn't reciprocity simple human decency? What this man failed to understand is that his view of the relationship was an arbitrary preconception. It was *his* image of what a relationship means. It was an assumption. As the American actor, comedian, writer, and director Henry Winkler (Fonzie in *Happy Days*) is quoted as saying, "Assumptions are the termites of relationships."

To succeed in any relationship, we have to rid ourselves of these arbitrary preconceived notions. Sometimes we get irritated if people don't measure up to our preconceived ideas of duty, responsibility, or even just what we think of as appropriate behavior. One such example from my own family life comes readily to mind. A few years ago, I became puzzled and concerned as to why my adult son hardly ever called me. I believed that children should call their parents frequently. But on reflection, I realized that was just my arbitrary assumption. After all, I had always encouraged my son to be independent. For example, when he was thirteen, I had allowed and supported his wish to travel with a friend from the United States to Germany to visit another friend. Independence and self-reliance are part of his makeup. When I got over my irritation and reflected on that fact, I realized the truth: his failure to call wasn't due in the slightest to a lack of care, thought, or love. The answer is simple: he doesn't share my assumption of what he *should* be doing to nurture our relationship.

After thinking about the issues he was having with his brother, the man in Mark's example gave up on the arbitrary notion that calling every week or two is part of the good-brother job description. Letting go of that assumption dramatically improved his mindset and his view of the relationship. Once he dropped that idea, it didn't make his brother call him more; he just didn't let it worry him. His earlier view no longer sat there like a festering false assumption. The conversations the brothers had following the man's realization were all the more engaging and meaningful.

Sometimes you get apologetic for reaching out to someone you haven't spoken to in a while. That's another example of having a fixed notion of what you should be doing for the relationship. It's quite likely the other person doesn't have the same set of expectations at all. Like the biblical prodigal son, he or she is just delighted to hear from you and is ready, able, and willing to engage in a meaningful way. Don't seek total reciprocity in any of your relationships; accept that people have different ideas and assumptions about nurturing a relationship. And always think of the end game—the objective. It's not some arbitrary notion of a call every week; it's to have a meaningful relationship that can nurture and sustain your life.

RULE 3: BE GENUINE

This is a cardinal rule. You cannot fake friendship or caring. If you try to cultivate friendship because you need something from someone or think it could benefit your career, you will always be found out. If you need from, say, someone you went to school with a job reference, a dentist's recommendation, or just suggestions for worthwhile activities in a city you're visiting, it's tempting to cultivate that friendship. How many times has someone you vaguely know or are three connections away from requested a LinkedIn connection? After a few upbeat too-familiar messages, the request comes: buy something, join something, recommend me, comment on my article. It's as transparent as a pane of glass.

One of the most demanding challenges is sustaining relationships when neither party needs anything from the other. But that's what being genuine is all about. In a 2016 *Forbes* article, author and emotional-intelligence guru Dr. Travis Bradberry highlighted what genuine people do. He related this to emotional intelligence, pointedly stating, "Emotional intelligence won't do a thing for you if you aren't genuine."[30]

Dr. Bradberry cited a University of Washington study that found that people are naturally skeptical—they don't accept emotional-intelligence demonstrations at face value. Emotional intelligence is a learned—and highly valuable—skill, but emotions have to be genuine. As humans, we are extremely good at sniffing that out. As Oscar Wilde famously said, "Be yourself; everybody else is taken."

I also find that telling people what you expect in one situation or another is very healthy. To me, this is part of being genuine. The way that I like to think about this is telling people directly what your expectation is when there is a mismatch between what happens and what you expected. One important way of doing this is to always use the word *I* to start every sentence: "I expected that this was going to be the outcome."

I once went into a business partnership with a friend. We bought a business, and we started to operate it. I quickly realized that his expectations and mine were different. No one was wrong. It was just that he expected me to do something and I expected we would run the business in a different way. Whenever we had conversations about our mutual missed expectations, I always talked about "I." In the end, we both realized we couldn't do business together because, quite frankly, his Me @ Work was different from my Me @ Work in this business. I sold the business to him, and we continued to be great friends. I learned from this that being direct had saved us a lot of uncomfortable situations.

RULE 4: THINK LONG-TERM: BUILD THE RELATIONSHIPS OF TOMORROW

I devoted chapter 1 to explaining why you should always make decisions with the future in mind. Just for a moment, step out of today's reality and envisage a future you. Don't let the relentless pressure

---

[30] *Forbes*, https://www.forbes.com/sites/travisbradberry/2016/05/10/12-habits-of-genuine-people/.

for instant gratification distract you from the fact that, although in retrospect life feels short, it's a marathon, not a sprint. Understand how you can make the journey so much more fulfilling by thinking about the me of tomorrow. The same applies to relationships. I've given you many reasons why you should care about the strength of your relationships. If you do, realize that they are jewels to be treasured, not broken glass to be tossed away.

I am lucky enough to have good relationships with my siblings, although just like any other family, we have our moments. Our serious conflicts have generally been few and far between, and they feel like sharp sticks in my memory. One such incident involves a furious argument I had with my older sister several decades ago. Tempers were raised, and harsh words were exchanged. It felt to me that our relationship was fraying. After we'd had a few conversations, it was clear we did not see eye to eye on a particular issue. In retrospect, I find it hard to imagine why it seemed so important. But just then, I was not in the mood to let it go.

Things were still boiling when one of my close friends gave me invaluable advice: *just drop it*. Think big picture: Is the issue worth more than your relationship? Think long-term: How will fighting over this issue now affect your relationship of tomorrow?

These kinds of issues are challenging. Weighing the importance of an issue versus the importance of a relationship in the heat of a quarrel is well-nigh impossible. The skill we need to learn is to step outside the problem, try to think about it objectively and dispassionately, and carefully weigh its value. Of course, you have to confront some issues. But sometimes (and this was such a time), the problem is not significant enough to jeopardize the long-term relationship that will be critical for the me of tomorrow.

To summarize, many relationships suffer or fail in one of two important ways:

- We fall out over a relatively unimportant issue.
- We fail to confront a really important issue out of fear of harming a relationship.

One way of illustrating this is in the following simple diagram (figure 7).

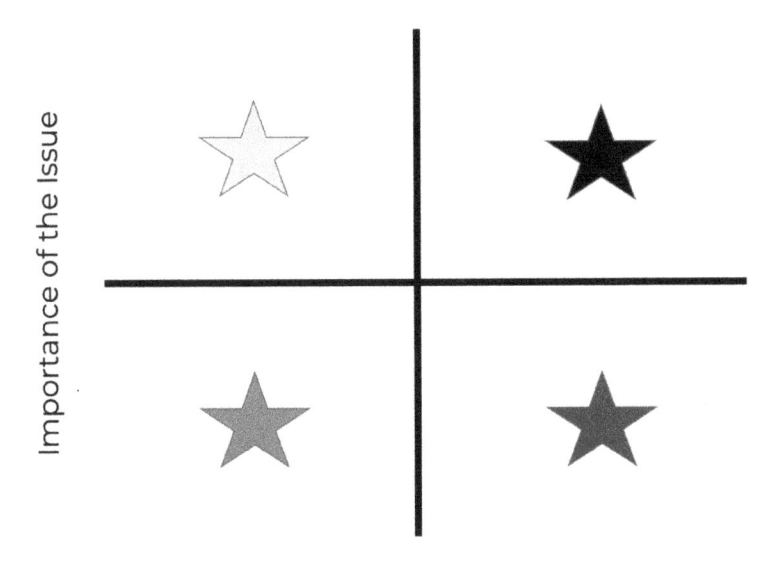

[Figure: A four-quadrant diagram. Vertical axis labeled "Importance of the Issue"; horizontal axis labeled "Importance of the Relationship". Top-left quadrant contains a white star; top-right a black star; bottom-left a light gray star; bottom-right a dark gray star.]

Importance of the Relationship

Figure 7.

The stars in this figure can be explained as follows:

1. Light gray stars (bottom left) represent simple transactions—maybe asking a barista the price of our coffee. This is not something worth stressing about.
2. A white star relationship (top left) might involve a car-purchase negotiation with a salesperson. The issue at hand is important, but we don't have a relationship we must build or preserve.
3. Dark-gray-star relationships (bottom right) often cause avoidable conflict. But if we grasp that the issue is less important than the relationship, we can defuse this conflict and maintain a healthy relationship. It's easy to clash with someone you're close to over an issue that in the greater scheme of life is really not that important. The lesson here

is that people often argue over issues without recognizing that those issues are nowhere near as important as the relationship itself. Psychologists tell us that sometimes the argument is a proxy for a deeper underlying issue—black stars (top right). But for many such conflicts, if we analyze an issue dispassionately, sometimes it's our own anger, fear, or stubbornness that generates much of the conflict.

When considering dark-gray-star issues, it's also important to remember that people rarely have the same perspective on the importance of an issue. It's like that age-old discussion of two people looking at a digit from different ends: one sees a six, the other a nine. Both people strongly believe they are right, and in a sense, they both are. But their perspectives are just different. Just because you believe you are right doesn't mean the other person is wrong.

4. Black stars (top right) signify the area of most significant challenge. Even if we understand, after dispassionate analysis, that the issue is important, our natural conflict-avoidance mechanism kicks in, and we often sidestep the issue. However, often, these are the very issues we need to embrace head-on. Avoiding them will further damage the relationship. Paradoxically, embracing such an issue not only addresses it and leads to a resolution but very often improves the overall relationship.

The best examples of these issues occur in spousal or close family relationships, where many areas of potential conflict rear their heads. A contentious issue will come to a boil at some point, and the potential for harm will be all the greater because of the past avoidance. Avoiding it will only put off conflict until later—like kicking the can down the road.

This quadrant is full of big, important issues, like the approach to family finances, how kids will be raised, and so forth. I remember the hugely consequential decision my wife and I made to move to the United States as newlyweds. She was a practicing dentist. Moving to a new country, with a new language, where she would require a long period of training and certification created serious challenges for her. She had already spent years of training and practice, and her career would stall. The importance of our relationship required that these challenges be acknowledged, the decision be explored from all angles, and the issue be addressed head-on. We could not avoid or postpone either the decision or her feelings regarding its impact.

This rule is clear: never let an unimportant issue cloud what's really much more important for the long term, the me of tomorrow—the relationship with your partner, child, friend, or coworker. Consequently, it's critical to clearly and dispassionately evaluate the importance of the issue that's causing conflict: know which ones are not worth fighting over and which you may have been avoiding. When critical issues are involved, don't skirt or avoid them. Dealing with them head-on usually strengthens the relationship. It prevents them from becoming a silent drain on relationship quality.

RULE 5: PROVIDE FEEDBACK THAT CAN BE HEARD

We exacerbate many relationship problems through poor communication. Sometimes we damage them terminally. Just as we strive to understand other people's points of view, they struggle just as much to understand ours. Even if we don't have the same assumptions about what constitutes good relationship behavior, it's critical to tell our friends, spouses, siblings, or children where we stand and what we value in those relationships.

However, there's a difference between stating your opinion and telling others how to run their lives. Even in the closest relationships—for example, with partners or children—you should try to avoid telling the other people what to do.

This may sound like a subtle difference, but it's an essential art—and one you need to practice. Offer advice and voice opinions, but never dictate what people should do. Don't ever claim "I told you so" when things don't turn out well. If someone asks you for advice, offer it, but not in a preachy or self-righteous manner.

One useful idea I've incorporated into my relationships came from a management training session I attended many years ago, run by a French agency called Là. Here is the most impactful slide (figure 8). It contains just a series of simple words. These simple little words act like magic. They are conflict deflectors, thought enhancers, and relationship savers.

The art of the feedback

I like +	I wish ...
I wonder ?	I have an idea !

Figure 8

One of the hardest things to understand and accept, especially with people we love deeply, is that they have to make their own mistakes. Personal mistakes are much more powerful teachers. Furthermore, as Jonathan Haidt explained so eloquently in his classic *The Righteous Mind*, arguing from the perspective of reason is often pointless.[31] When making moral decisions, human beings use intuition first and strategic reasoning second, often as ex post justification for decisions

---

[31] Jonathan Haidt, *The Righteous Mind: Why Good People Are Divided by Politics and Religion* (New York: Pantheon Books, 2012).

they've already made. We can't make people "see reason": we're not wired that way. We also need to understand our differences—what works for us may not work for them.

UNIQUE RELATIONSHIPS: THE FAMILY

As the adage (sometimes attributed to Harper Lee) says, "You can choose your friends, but you can't choose your family." Family relationships are the most long-lasting, sturdy, and emotionally challenging relationships we have. While my five rules apply equally to these relationships, there are special considerations in addition to these general rules.

SPOUSE OR PARTNER

We know that marriage rates and commitment to a life partner in the US are in decline. Earlier, I referred to the National Opinion Research Center data showing a 25 percent decrease in the number of people in marriage or life partnerships since the mid-1980s. A decade ago, the Pew Research Center published data that showed stark attitudinal differences among people based on age. Almost half of those under thirty agreed with statements such as "marriage is becoming obsolete," "new family arrangements are a good thing," and "children don't need a mother and father to grow up happily," versus one-third of those over fifty.

Now, we can see how those attitudes have turned into behaviors. Data from the Centers for Disease Control and Prevention (CDC) and the National Center for Health Statistics shows that the marriage rate per one thousand people has fallen steadily from 8.2 in 2000 to 6.5 in 2018. Actually, divorce rates show a parallel decline, suggesting that people *may* be taking more time and becoming more discerning about their selection of life partners. However, 782,038 divorces versus 2,132,853 marriages in 2018 show that the real number of divorces remains high.[32]

Theories for these trends abound. Some cite the growing income gap. There are fewer financially stable partners available in more deprived communities. Others point to a broader change in public attitudes toward this millennia-old institution and more women in the workforce. In a recent survey, Pew reported that Americans were more likely to cite career enjoyment than marriage as the key to a fulfilling life.[33]

While these statistics show a continuing trend away from the spouse or partner relationship, we can't ignore that 1:1 personal relationships remain paramount for many people. That same Pew survey showed that 86 percent described being in a committed romantic relationship as either essential or important to living a fulfilling life, for both men and women. In a world overflowing with marriage advice, it can seem hard to find useful nuggets. In this most intimate of relationships, few hold the keys to wisdom.

An arena so influenced by emotion makes it especially hard to navigate with the tools of reason. However, in my experience, there are a few simple pointers for helping us develop and nurture this special relationship.

1. **The loving person.** Early in a relationship, it's essential not to let the heart rule the head. Take time to find the right person, and as I advise in chapter 1, think about the me of tomorrow when making a commitment, especially one as consequential as this. Another element I have found valuable is to find out as much as possible about your potential partner and the state of his or her other close life relationships. I describe it as looking for a *loving person* as a partner rather than

---

[32] CDC National Center for Health Statistics, https://www.cdc.gov/nchs/nvss/marriage-divorce.htm.

[33] https://www.pewresearch.org/fact-tank/2020/02/14/more-than-half-of-americans-say-marriage-is-important-but-not-essential-to-leading-a-fulfilling-life/.

just a partner you are *in love with*. This is a concept I heard during a speech while in college, and it stuck with me. The presenter stated unequivocally, "It is as important to marry a loving person as it is to marry someone that is in love with you." Whatever the level of mutual love you feel going into a long-term commitment, there will always be problems. Relationships never follow an even path. Nothing ever goes smoothly. However, if you have selected a genuinely loving partner, it will be much easier to work through these problems. Understand how your partner treats people and balances his or her desires with the needs and desires of others. My daughter told me about a simple test for this. It's not infallible, but it's a good start. If you are having dinner with a date, watch how that person treats the waitstaff. If your date is kind and considerate, especially if there are problems, that gives you a clue.

2. **Men and women.** For those in heterosexual relationships, failing to appreciate basic gender-based needs can lead you astray. Alongside all other needs, I have found one consistent truism: men seek respect, and women seek love. Admittedly, this covers a multitude of sins, but one ignores these fundamental differences, socially conditioned or not, at one's peril. One of the books I particularly like that elaborates this point is *Love and Respect* by Dr. Emerson Eggerichs. My wife and I read this book together after ten or so years of marriage. She was participating in a seminar, and a speaker suggested it. At first, I was reluctant to read the book, but my wife was persistent, and I relented. I learned quite a bit from it, and it helped me frame my needs as a husband and hers as a wife. I love it. There's many a word to live by in it.[34]

3. **Modeling.** Those of us lucky enough to have children know that they come with a whole new set of challenges, some of

---

[34] Emerson Eggerichs, *Love and Respect: The Love She Most Desires, the Respect He Desperately Needs* (Nashville: Integrity Publishers, 2004).

which I'll touch on in the next section. We should never allow ourselves to forget: children start their relationship education from us and our partners. It's an excellent education for young impressionable minds to see a couple handling challenges in a mature, responsible way; looking to build and strengthen the relationship; and focusing on the relationship rather than the issue. Daughters will look at the relationship the mother has with the father and say, "That's what a wife should do in a marriage." Sons will look at the behavior of the father with the mother and conclude, "That's how a husband has to behave with his wife." Like the old adage suggests, they will learn from what they see and not from what they are told.

4. **Reciprocity.** You hear a lot about *reciprocity* in spousal relationships. I think we often misunderstand the term. Reciprocity doesn't mean that you take turns washing the dishes or cooking dinner; it's much more nuanced than that. Discuss how you can best support each other in the roles you have in life—physically, emotionally, and practically.

CHILDREN

Some of you don't have children and may have no plans for them. If so, this brief sojourn into parent-child relationships may not be for you. However, I could argue that in the spirit of "It takes a village," child development is really a shared responsibility for all responsible adults. However, that responsibility is so much more immediate and keenly felt by parents themselves. Hence, if you're not a parent and never plan to be, feel free to skip this short section.

There are libraries full of literature about how to raise children. I've never met a parent who doesn't own at least five books on the subject. Ever since I became a father almost twenty-five years ago, it's been a subject I've explored deeply, discussed avidly, and written about often. But I claim no particular expertise. Nor do I have any unique insight into child psychology. All parents are lifetime students; provided we keep our eyes and ears open, we can keep learning. However, when it comes to the relationship part of dealing with children, I offer a few nuggets for you to keep at the front of your mind in building nurturing relationships as children age.

It's not always evident when you first become a parent that your little children will only be that for a blink of an eye. Your offspring will be adults for much longer than they are children: consequently, it's important to think early about values that adults need. This is true me-of-tomorrow thinking. And if you're fortunate, your relationship with them as coadults will be longer than the adult-child relationship you share. During the adult-child period of my relationship with my kids, I wanted to help them establish what I considered to be essential tools for life: a work ethic, independence and confidence, an understanding of reward systems for accomplishments, a positive mindset, accountability for mistakes and the rejection of excuses, and the love of lifetime learning that I discussed in chapter 3.

Usually, separation—a process that starts early and accelerates through the teenage years—brings the toughest relationship challenges. This makes it all the more vital that you take advantage of those early years to build and nurture your relationship and communicate your values. A good relationship in the early years requires a blend of guidance and independence, a combination that's so difficult to balance. My friend Charlie once told me that by the time your children are fourteen or so, you are done teaching them. He claimed that you only have from about age nine to fourteen to teach them the right values and behavior because, at that age, they will listen. By the time children reach age fourteen, they start to pull away. You should aim to keep a healthy close relationship, but it won't be anything like before. This is OK. This is nature's way of preparing them for independence once Mom and Dad are no longer around. They won't necessarily agree with the advice you offer, but they will listen. They will know where you stand and likely keep the information tucked away in the back of their rebellious minds.

For me, the hardest part of parenting was watching my children make decisions that I knew were wrong. On the one hand, I wanted to spare them disappointments, but on the other hand, I knew that making mistakes was the best way for them to learn. I still remember vividly arguing with my fifteen-year-old son about why practicing math problems helps you get better grades. He told me I was wrong many times. He used to say to me that math was something you either understood or you didn't, and he assured me he did. It wasn't the age for him to recognize that practice makes perfect.

The good news is that although you think you've lost your children at fourteen, all being well, they will come back, this time as adults. And although the new relationship is adult to adult, as long as you recognize and respect that change and treat your children like the responsible adults they are, your new connection will be fruitful and productive.

One basic rule in parenting is that you need to think long-term. Children need to be independent; they need to learn from their mistakes.

As long as it doesn't do them serious harm, let them make mistakes. And never say, "I told you so!" Instead, tell them that learning from mistakes is hard and that although, right now, it hurts or feels wrong, the good news is they will appreciate it later. The way you handle their friendships is also important. It's rarely productive to question or criticize your kids' choice of friends. Instead, say something along the lines of "If I were you, I would be careful with [A or B person or C or D situation]."

It's essential to help children build resilience. Remember that they won't be with us all the time, and we want them to be ready for life instead of thinking that we can always take care of them.

SPECIAL RELATIONSHIPS: FRIENDS

I'm a great believer in close friendships. I think of my closest friends as siblings. As author Simon Sinek said, "Good friends make us better people. They cheer us when we hit bottom and keep us humble when we reach the top." However, as the volume of literature on friendship attests, these unique relationships bring their own particular problems.

The first group of problems surrounds friend selection. Usually, when we are children, this comes naturally. Like the women on Okinawa Island, some people are lucky enough to have lifetime friends they stay in touch with and grow together with. I am fortunate in this respect: every week, I keep up with my four closest buddies from high school; in many ways, we relate to one another as if we are still fifteen years old. Nothing much has changed about how we treat one another, tease one another, and laugh. However, I'm acutely conscious that not all of us have had the same luck in life. But at its heart, that doesn't seem to matter so much. In a transitory and intensely mobile society like that of the US, relationships this long are rare. Even good friendships that people establish in their college years tend to slowly dissolve.

When you live different lifestyles, in other places, with various pressures, it becomes hard to relate—hence many a fractured relationship. A 2019 study of American social dynamics, conducted by OnePoll and published by Evite, reveals the struggles Americans have with establishing friendships. Their survey of two thousand adults shows that the average American hasn't made a new friend in five years, has only three best friends, and only five good friends. High school still remains the place where almost half of American friendships are forged.

The data also shows that despite the proliferation of digital friendships, people clearly distinguish between digital and real friends. They discriminate in selecting friends and have a high bar for what they consider to be real friends. It remains true that friends are the family we choose.

The second set of issues relates to the problems of comparison and competition. Most of us have friends who have been conventionally more successful than us, perhaps financially, professionally, or in terms of civic accomplishments. Especially with friends from high school or college, it's hard not to make comparisons and to compete.

That's one reason so many people eschew high school reunions. However, true friendship reaches through this veil.

I've always believed that the mark of a true friend is someone who genuinely wishes you success, without a trace of jealousy, and someone for whom you sincerely hope every success, equally jealousy-free.

I feel especially lucky because I came to work in an organization filled with international transplants like me. Since many of us were in a different land with only our immediate families, we developed strong relationships—so strong that some felt like family. Because of my close high school friendships, I was conditioned to think that the most intimate friendships are those established early in life; however, my new work situation taught me that it is possible to develop new sincere close friendships even later in life. Work eventually split a few of us, but that didn't stop us from seeing each other when travel took one of us to another's new hometown. I have been to the weddings of some of these friends' children, and our spouses also talk with one another.

SPECIAL RELATIONSHIPS: PROFESSIONAL OR WORK

In many ways, building and nurturing professional relationships can be more challenging than sustaining intimate family and friend relationships. First, I should give a quick nod to boundaries. Happily, this is much less of an issue than it was in my early days in corporate America. While some office friendships go beyond friendship, by now, we are all well aware of the hazards of office romance, mixed signals, and sexual harassment. We have all moved a long way forward from when the head of HR at my global Fortune 100 company resigned after persistent stories of workplace indiscretion. Professional relationships are just that: professional. We build them to support and strengthen us (and other people) in that vital work sphere of our lives.

These issues aside, professional relationships can be perplexing.

One problem is that many people see them as transactional. I mentioned earlier the apparent insincerity of those LinkedIn users who randomly ask to connect, only to follow up after a less-than-discreet pause with a request or a sales pitch. Their behavior screams that they want a transaction, not a relationship, and they often want the worst trade of all: something for nothing! LinkedIn may be one of the best business-networking, lead-generation, and career-development tools around, but we should never confuse these functions with genuine relationships. Genuine relationships are with people with whom we have a connection and real interest—people we like to spend time with and learn from and who provide knowledge and advice in return. Another problem with this type of relationship—and here I would also include those interactions on social media platforms like Facebook and Instagram—is that it can confuse easy, almost thoughtless connection with genuine care. How much effort and forethought does it take to add your five-word greeting to the sixty-three others acknowledging someone's birthday?

However, I can't deny that the primary purpose of professional relationships is mutual benefit. Your time at work is valuable and (as I argue in chapter 2) should be strictly bounded. Nobody has time to build professional relationships with everyone he or she comes into contact with. So even though you shouldn't pursue purely transactional relationships, you should still seek relationships with people based on mutual benefit. But you need to choose those people carefully. Whom you choose will impact your work life and career opportunities in the future. Many hiring studies dramatically illustrate the importance of networking for career advancement: up to 75 percent of professionals leveraged their existing networks to uncover their latest opportunities. So while professional relationships should not be transactional, we all understand them as sources of immediate and mutual benefit. These relationships represent invaluable networks.

CHOOSING YOUR NETWORK

As long as your relationship intention is genuine and there is no immediate transactional intent on either side, professional associations are mutually enriching. I've built relationships with literally dozens of former colleagues, customers, and business partners, many of these people I now classify as personal friends. That takes them into a different category altogether.

One of the simplest ways to evaluate and analyze your current network is to build a matrix like the one illustrated in figure 9. Map your connections into this matrix as objectively as you can. These links are not static—people will migrate across quadrants as your career develops or you learn more about them. But it gives you a place to start and a focus as to which connections you should spend your time with.

A word of explanation—these dimensions are personal subjective judgments:

- **Strong versus weak.** This is your assessment of the depth of connection you feel with a person.

    This designation isn't necessarily about whether you regularly talk to someone or send him or her birthday or holiday greetings. It can be based on a unique shared experience—maybe just a moment—that you feel confident this person will recall just as quickly as you.

    I remember meeting colleagues at training classes or leadership gatherings or working with them on special projects. Thrown together to create a presentation or meet a deadline, we worked closely and intensely, and in the process, we got to know one another's strengths and weaknesses and maybe our dreams and ambitions. Business travel to unusual places with a colleague can have the same impact, even if you never work together again.

The more intense the experience, the longer that strong connection lasts. For a brief time, you become comrades in arms.

- **Relevant versus irrelevant.** This classification relates to your purpose and objectives. You might have a powerful connection, but the other person's knowledge, expertise, and current working situation make him or her less relevant for your *current* connection goals. That doesn't mean this person won't become relevant in the future—circumstances change—but for the time being, he or she belongs in the upper-left quadrant.

    Conversely, you might have had occasional contact with someone who is now in an extremely relevant role for your career goal, whether you're seeking information, a new position, or strategic guidance. This person is in the bottom-right quadrant.

    The sweet spot for this matrix is the top-right quadrant. However, it's always worth building a complete map so you can see it dynamically. People you know may have changed companies, roles, and skills sets. The last thing to assume is that people's career paths are static, even if yours feels that way at certain times.

    Career development often happens in fits and starts; that junior account executive you worked with three years ago might now be a marketing-communications lead in a totally different industry. The reverse of this happened to me. I was in hardware development for many years before transitioning to software. Over the next few years, former colleagues would sometimes call me to help them search for an engineer or marketing professional, but I was no longer relevant to them in that sense. They were unaware that I had changed industries.

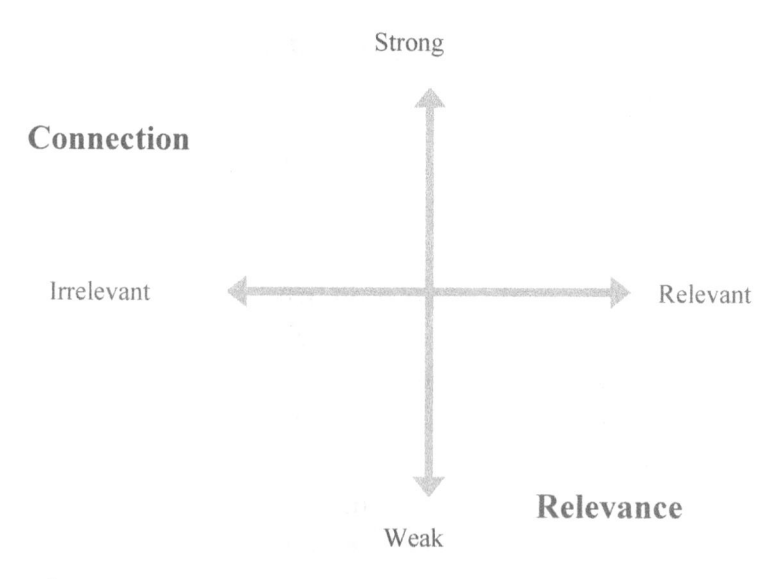

```
              Strong
                ↑
 **Connection** |
                |
 Irrelevant ←———+———→ Relevant
                |
                |      **Relevance**
                ↓
              Weak
```

Figure 9.

Most of the people in my network are not even in industries or positions I would typically interact with. Some are people I worked closely with but who have since moved to different places, industries, or professions. The professional world, like your own career, is dynamic. However, it's always a pleasant surprise when old contacts show up in the right places, where you least expect to see them. Of course, this will only help you if you have maintained and nurtured the relationships. They will not be there for you, or you for them, if there have been no continuing relationships. And just as with all the other relationships I've discussed, the core relationship rules apply:

- Understand yourself (and what you want from the connection).
- Abandon any preconceptions.
- Be genuine.
- Think long-term.
- Always provide feedback in the right way.

STRATEGIES TO BUILD YOUR NETWORK

Besides choosing which of your current contacts to focus on, you will need some strategies to add to your list. Sometimes, new professional relationships present themselves: coworkers; people you have built personal connections with though day-to-day interaction; and people you know through one of life's other domains, such as college friends or social contacts who are also building professional relationships, all come to mind.

Many experts recommend attending local chapters of professional societies. These can be valuable, although you should select new contacts with care: some people actively participate in these groups seeking that occasional transactional relationship, like for a new job or sales opportunity.

Today's networking tools make identifying and selecting potential networking partners both informed and targetable. However, that's just the first part of the exercise. Deciding on which relationships you want to invest in wholeheartedly is essential. Don't discard a potential contact too soon or persist with pursuing one if there's no genuine commonality of interest.

If you work in a large company with employees in many far-flung places and remote locations, look for people in your company, perhaps in a different geography, who do similar jobs and have a comparable business background. The outreach should go beyond sending a LinkedIn connection request. Tell such a person that you do a similar job and are looking to compare notes and share best practices.

If you work in a small company, the approach can be similar. In this case, seek out people from other companies who appear to do a similar job, obviously recognizing and avoiding any competitive risks.

Like in business development, identifying new contacts, leveraging existing relationships to help reach them, and building your network is time consuming. It requires focus and dedication. Always remember there has to be mutual interest and sufficient professional overlap to make the relationship professionally worthwhile for both parties.

NETWORKING RULES

As I mentioned, my five relationship rules apply in equal measure to professional relationships and to family and friends. Think of these rules as the base-level keys to any successful relationship. In the case of professional-relationship development, here are some other rules I would add:

- **Always seek to add value.** No productive professional relationship can be all give and no take. If you stumble across interesting, relevant content for your connections, pass it on. A light but useful touch goes a long way. Don't immediately ask for favors, preferment, or recommendations; just listen, support, and encourage the relationship. We learn and grow from listening to other people. You'll be surprised how often conversations yield much more than you expected.
- **Establish a mutual interest.** As you exchange ideas and information, make sure there is a commonality of interest. This is easy if you are in the same company, but it's also valuable to network with people with different roles in the same industry or with similar positions in an entirely different one. You can only successfully network with people who are as interested in a relationship with you as you are with them.
- **Nurture people who lose their jobs.** Especially in good times, many people assume those who lose their jobs are suddenly untouchable. It's as if they've fallen off a cliff. Data consistently shows how much easier it is to get hired when you already have a job. For various reasons, employers show consistent bias against people on the outside. When people in my network lose or even just change their jobs, I offer sincere support and advice. If they've been unlucky enough

to be laid off—and luck does play a considerable part in this—they often need someone to talk to and bounce ideas off and someone with whom they can develop a strategy for finding their next roles. People never forget the consideration and kindness of gestures like this, and they willingly reciprocate when fortunes are reversed.

- **Befriend the person, not the title.** People have one of two reactions to networking with people with senior roles or maybe just senior-sounding titles. Some see them as targets to aim for—well-connected people who can accelerate their careers. Others are intimidated, thinking, for example, that such a busy executive will have no time for them. Both of these reactions are wrong. Evaluate the relationship based on shared mutual interest and benefit. Even busy executives—if they're truth seekers—have time to hear a different perspective from someone without an ax to grind. But if you're interested in the relationship because of the person's status and title, it will soon become apparent; it's visible a thousand miles away. Typically, close networking relationships with senior executives are based on mutual interest, prior contact, or personal experience. It's never a successful strategy to fill your network with senior people with whom you have weak connections just because there's a chance they'll be especially helpful to you.

- **Go deep, not broad.** Some people pride themselves on the number of their connections. But none of us has enough time or energy to nurture a large number of contacts. Like those five-word birthday greetings on Facebook, a superficial relationship is hardly better than no connection at all. By all means, become a LinkedIn superconnector (defined as more than one thousand first-level connections), but don't mistake these connections for professional relationships. It's more effective to build and foster a manageable number of meaningful relationships than to construct a thousand-person LinkedIn network.

Maintaining this level of networking activity will dilute your focus. You'll end up with the worst of both worlds: few genuine connections because there's no time to nurture them and many connections to those with whom you don't have real relationships. Keep in touch with your professional colleagues—not just through LinkedIn (although liking their articles and posts can never hurt).

Maintain contact, *especially* when you don't need anything, though maybe you don't have anything special to share. In his book *Advocacy: Championing Ideas and Influencing Others,* University of Texas professor John Daly describes how he starts every New Year by contacting some of those in his professional network, telling them that his New Year's resolution is to reach out and just find out how they're doing.[35] This kind of unsolicited approach builds trust and enthusiasm. And it goes without saying that a personal birthday message is way more impactful than those five words on Facebook!

- **Remember the importance of weak connections.** Mark Granovetter in "The Strength of Weak Ties" teaches us all about it.[36] We all have relationships with people, often close colleagues, with whom we talk to almost every day. We know what they're thinking and feeling, and they are always top of mind when we think of our work domain. Besides, we have established, well-nurtured, genuine professional relationships with people who, for one reason or another, we don't connect with often. Perhaps it's their preferred relationship style or maybe just that our professional paths don't cross as they once did.

    For want of a better word, I would call these *weak* connections. Just to be clear, this weakness is one of frequency and continuity, not a reflection of the strength of our relationships or our ability to resurrect closer connections.

---

[35] John A. Daly, *Advocacy: Championing Ideas and Influencing Others* (New Haven: Yale University Press, 2011).

[36] Mark S. Granovetter, "The Strength of Weak Ties," *American Journal of Sociology* 78, no. 6 (1973): 1360–80, https://doi.org/10.1086/225469.

Because of this lack of contact frequency, these people are not top of mind to us, nor we to them. If we had a new opportunity or a critical piece of information to share, these are not the people we would immediately think of, and vice versa.

However, these connections are essential: we have invested time and effort to build the relationships. We need to remember to nurture and connect with these people. In our enthusiasm for our strong professional relationships, we must not forget to cultivate those weak ones.

RELATIONSHIP EXERCISE

We all have the desire to improve certain relationships in the abstract. However, most of us rarely take the time to explore our relationships systematically. Sometimes we let them deteriorate or drift, or we just ignore emerging signs of disconnection. If you have such unique relationships—be they familial, friendly, or collegial—this exercise can help you get things back on track:

1. Choose somebody with whom you want to improve your relationship. It's best to start with someone with whom you have a shared familiarity and history—don't apply this plan to a budding romance!
2. In the spirit of rule 1, "Understand yourself," do one of the personality tests outlined earlier in the chapter. MBTI is probably the quickest and easiest. There are simple online options available.
3. Ask the other person if he or she knows his or her MBTI (or DISC or Enneagram, if that's your choice) type. If not, send the person a link, and ask that he or she take the test. Most people are usually willing to embark on a short voyage of self-discovery.

4. Compare your typologies. Use the decoding tools available for each test to understand the differences in outlook and behavior between your type and that of the other person.
5. Assess the extent to which the relationship problem is related to differences in type. A type conflict doesn't mean the relationship is doomed. There are no *best* combinations of types in relationships. But applying type or category theory to relationships will provide you with some key insights—for example, how the other person deals with conflict, makes decisions, draws his or her energy, and engages in activities.
6. In future dealings with your friend, partner, or colleague, keep these differences in mind. Adjust your approach to reflect these differences. If you want to go deep, all these personality typologies have tool kits that can help you understand how best to change your approach to engage that person better. If the other person is so inclined, you can give him or her gentle advice on dealing with you better.

There's one other consideration in a relationship conflict that's especially pertinent in today's politically charged environment. Many relationships fracture over political, religious, or moral questions. These fractures are hard to fix and nearby impossible to ignore. If your conflict has this essential element, the only advice I can offer is to read Jonathan Haidt's *The Righteous Mind*, referenced earlier. Understanding how people arrive at moral decisions and use reasoning to justify their political or ethical positions arms you with what not to say or do to exacerbate that conflict.

A combination of using personality type and understanding moral reasoning will go a long way to helping you solve relationship problems. And it's an excellent first step to developing an understanding of personality and relationship differences.

CONCLUSION

In many ways, this has been the most challenging chapter to write. As someone who loves data, frameworks, analysis, systems, processes, targets, and goals, relationships sometimes feel fluid, fungible, and amorphous. They are hard to define and analyze. Connections between and among people can't easily be summarized in spreadsheets or PowerPoint presentations. However, for two particular reasons, building relationships might be the most crucial element of building your me of tomorrow.

First, understanding and nurturing human relationships is critical for success in business and in life. While you can enjoy superficial success without them, they are as essential as the air we breathe. They make us live longer, happier, more fulfilled lives. In all of life's domains, meaningful relationships are the essence of success.

Secondly, on a personal note, relationships have been the fuel of my life and remain so today. They are endlessly fascinating, perplexing, sometimes frustrating, but never dull. Personal relationships are the vehicle through which we can all make the most impact on the world. I'm sure you will have the same experience.

CHAPTER 5

ME @ WORK: BUILDING A VALUABLE CAREER

I am not a product of my circumstances. I am a product of my decisions.

—STEPHEN COVEY

The key to successful leadership is influence, not authority.

KEN BLANCHARD

If you've read up to here, you should have some new ideas to make your life more efficient and fulfilling. I wrote about the importance of planning for tomorrow; how allocating your energy across life's five domains provides real balance; and, crucially, how the best thing you can do for yourself is to become a lifelong learner, a truth seeker, always open to new ideas, methods, and information. I also discussed the importance of relationships and how to build a thriving professional network. This chapter builds on the last element, focusing on one crucial dimension of life: our work and the Me @ Work.

WHY AM I WORKING SO HARD AND GETTING NOWHERE?

It's one of the oldest American myths: hard work pays off. The clichés are everywhere: 1 percent inspiration, 99 percent perspiration; keep working hard, and you can get anything you want; there is no substitute for working hard; I learned the value of hard work by working hard; and—one of my favorites, attributed to Thomas Jefferson—"I'm a great believer in luck, and I find the harder I work, the more I have of it."

Please don't misunderstand me: I believe in hard work. Once you've identified goals, you should use as much energy and dedication as you can to achieve them. Many of these sayings have more than a grain of truth. But in my experience, hard work *alone* is never enough to build a career, advance in an organization, or be effective at work. I know many dedicated workers, smart and talented men and women, who go above and beyond the call of duty but languish in the corporate undergrowth. So if you feel underappreciated, you're not alone.

Sometimes, when we reflect on our careers, we know instinctively that we should be doing things differently to get ahead. Perhaps you've read books, attended seminars, and even employed a career coach. All these are worthwhile ideas. However, what you're likely missing is a simple formula: a set of tools you can use to make sense of this challenge. That's what this chapter aims to provide.

Many people talk about working smarter, not harder. I will show you how to be more effective at work, whatever it is you do, by building influence and relevance, my preferred path to career success. I will include a simple set of exercises to hone the soft skills essential for career success and fulfillment. These are skills that organizations, both large and small, value highly. They are often more valued than the technical or functional skills you build every day at work. This chapter also encourages you to examine your core motivations and to balance Me @ Work with life's other four dimensions: self, family, community and friendship, and spirituality.

As we develop their careers, we look for visible manifestations of progress. These show themselves in raises, promotions, titles, and increasing responsibility. However, I'm going to suggest a different metric for career progress that will set you up for longer-term success. This measure is the power of influence. First, I will talk about what this means.

THE POWER OF INFLUENCE

This section may contain the most critical advice for you to further your career. As we advance, we tend to chase titles and status. Because these achievements seem tangible, they become a cause for celebration. We feel we are finally getting somewhere, being recognized. These rewards are welcome. However, a better strategy for measuring long-term career development is chasing *influence.*

Look at the chart (figure 10) that I developed with my friend Cesar. One day, he came into my office after attending a management training class, flushed with this new idea: to measure the degree of influence in organizations. At that time, my colleague was an eager young professional trying to get ahead. He often talked somewhat negatively about his career. Cesar argued that the surest path to career success was to be a better "politician." He joked that "butt-kissing" was how you got ahead and landed a promotion. He used examples of people with high levels of responsibility and observed how close they were to the organization's leadership. Together, we more or less drew this chart. It aligns perfectly with what I've observed time and time again throughout my career. Understanding this was Cesar's eureka moment, and it's been a cornerstone of my thinking ever since.

The axes in figure 10 indicate degree of influence (x axis) and title or rank in the organization (y axis). To illustrate the point, think about two people in any large organization, represented by the 4- and 5-pointed stars.

Figure 10.

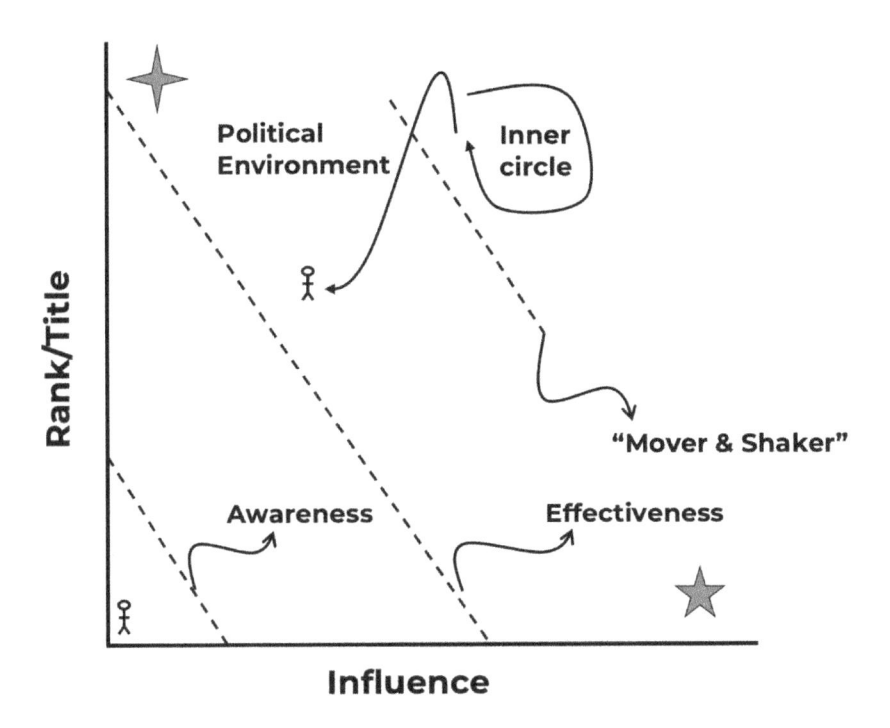

Rank/Title (y-axis) vs **Influence** (x-axis)

- Political Environment
- Inner circle
- "Mover & Shaker"
- Awareness
- Effectiveness

The 5-pointed star is the executive assistant to the CEO or division leader. This person often has a high degree of influence. Let's say the assistant is a woman. She often decides who gets access to the CEO. The CEO relies on her to make time trade-offs. However, she doesn't usually have a fancy title or a rank in the organization, often managing nobody. So she has a high influence and low rank or title.

The second person is at the other extreme and represented by the four-pointed star. Many companies have senior executives who were passed over in the last couple of rounds of promotions. Perhaps they were even in line for the CEO's job once but another candidate was chosen for whatever reason. These executives are usually assigned to "special projects" (i.e., interesting but lower-priority ideas) and tucked far away from the core of the business. Famously, Japanese companies deal with older executives this way when they are no longer needed. They are kept around so they can save face. This person has a high rank or title but little to no influence in the organization.

What we are exploring here is everything in between. Think of your career path and your organization as something like this: When you first started at your company, perhaps fresh out of college, you had little or no influence and certainly no grand title. Maybe you were an entry-level financial analyst, marketer, engineer, or sales representative. You didn't understand who anyone was or how to get much done. You could barely find your way to the company parking lot every morning or figure out where to go for lunch.

After a few months, you started to understand who your boss's manager was and maybe even her manager's manager. You understood what was expected of you, and people started coming to you for answers in your specific area. You continued to navigate the company jungle until, one day, you were promoted to the next grade level and paid a little more. Suddenly, you started to understand that there was a larger world out there. That day, you crossed the *awareness line*.

Over time, you continued to develop at your company and received more promotions and more money. Then you got to participate in meetings with your organization's leadership and perhaps presented to them on specific topics every once in a while. You knew where to go to get things done. You became effective. Without consciously knowing, you crossed the *effectiveness line*.

Once you crossed this line, you became part of the *political environment*. This was Cesar's eureka moment. It dawned on him that when people talk about "office politics," what they really mean is being part of an environment where people know how to get things done. They know which people need to be assigned to which projects to ensure they get completed on time. They know where to go for answers to tricky questions and whom to invite to meetings for their knowledge (and influence). Often, people in the political environment reach back to colleagues behind the effectiveness line to get stuff done. Many of the folks behind the effectiveness line work for people who are part of the political environment.

There is one more line beyond the political environment: the *mover and shaker line*. This line separates the political environment from the inner circle. People in the inner circle lead the organization. The inner circle usually comprises at least two individuals, but sometimes there are several more. The inner circle always includes the leader of the organization. Although people don't actually list *inner circle* in their job titles, these people know who they are.

The inner circle becomes the sounding board for the organization's leader. People in the inner circle alert the leader to issues that need to be addressed first. They are often responsible for finding answers to these issues. People in the inner circle reach to the political environment for answers, and people in the political environment either provide the solutions immediately or go away and get those answers from other people behind the effectiveness line. I have found this to be a nice shorthand for how most organizations work.

This type of arrangement works for many organizations, both large and small. You can also map a single department's political environment in this manner. That is, the marketing team may have a graph of its own in which the marketing manager is in the top right-hand corner, but that marketing manager may or may not be part of the larger organization's inner circle when the whole business gets mapped.

There are several things about this arrangement that may be counterintuitive. One is that an individual does not necessarily need to report directly to the organization leader in order to be part of the inner circle. There are people outside the leadership staff who get asked by the organization leader or others in the inner circle to shape the organization's direction and strategy. In short, they have the ear of the inner circle. They almost belong there. You can identify them by how often the organization leader asks them questions directly. You often see them attending meetings with members of the inner circle. Heck, they may be sitting with the organization's leader at lunchtime. If the leader listens to what they have to say, they are shaping her opinions.

I know a young executive to whom this applies perfectly. She sits three levels below the inner circle in a growing start-up. Yet time and time again, the leadership team calls her and asks her opinion. She is nearly always vocal and opinionated—almost always has something relevant to offer. This had become so evident that after a recent meeting, the CEO asked why she had been so quiet. He was concerned that she had not offered an opinion. She is a real influencer.

When people like this don't have high titles or ranks, it's almost certain that the organization will end up giving the designations to them anyway. It's incongruous when someone with such a significant influence helps shape the organization's strategy but lacks the title and authority of people in the inner circle. Even if such people seem content with their statuses, they become hard to justify. These people see no change in influence, but when the time is right, their titles change: they move straight up from the bottom right to the top right on the graph.

I've seen this play out in many organizations. One of the most memorable examples involves a colleague who worked in a multibillion-dollar division's strategic planning department. He came in as a manager, working on strategic issues with a staff of just two or three people. Very quickly, everyone knew he was the go-to guy for big ideas and strategic input. His fingerprints were on several new initiatives pursued by the division leader. He attended every quarterly business review, was often seen with members of the inner circle, and was clearly punching way above his weight. But still, he remained a manager, with a small staff. Then, suddenly, the division leader realized the paradox of his position. She promoted him to director and then, almost immediately, to VP. His title caught up with his influence. He didn't need to lobby for a promotion; after a while, she just knew it was necessary. The contradiction was apparent to everyone. He had become too important to ignore or to lose.

I firmly believe that seeking influence is a better career strategy than directly pursuing rank or title. Influence trumps position and title every time. Rest assured—once you have influence, position and money will follow. Just be patient and keep asserting that influence. No organization can have someone with significant influence and a low title for too long. It just doesn't make sense.

There is another important side note to this. If you are title focused, your peers and others can't fail to notice. Once they believe your rank and title exceeds your influence and value (i.e., you're in the top-left area of the chart), inevitably, they will help and support you less. Despite your title, they know you're less connected to the inner circle, less valuable to the organization in terms of knowing how to get things done, and, hence, of less use to colleagues who are trying to establish their influence. So if influence is critical, you may ask, "How do I build it?"

Let's take a look at some of the values that I have found people need to exhibit to become effective and influential in the organization.

ADDING VALUE TO ORGANIZATIONS

In simple terms, people who add the most value usually become successful and influential in organizations. However, understanding what your unique organization (or your part of it) values is nontrivial.

DEFINING VALUE

Value is easier to define for some functions than it is for others. For example, salespeople become more valuable by selling more! However, when you work across a matrix organization, with multiple people at different levels and in disparate places, knowing how to add more value is more complicated.

People in companies, especially large ones, are still divided roughly into three groups:

1. People who build the products or services

2. People who sell those products or services
3. People who sit between the first two groups, supporting one or both of these core functions in one way or another (there are many roles in this amorphous middle)

Over a long career, you will likely spend some time in all three of these groups. When you are in group 3—that amorphous middle—you need to identify how you can help either of the other two kinds of people. That's where the most obvious value resides. While your group 3 job may seem removed from the fray of building and selling, it's essential to keep the interests of groups 1 and 2 top of mind. If possible, put yourself into their shoes. Work out how your role can directly contribute to one or both of these critical constituencies.

Of course, work is not just about developing soft attributes and influencing leaders, as I discussed earlier. And while you look to understand where you can add the most value, never neglect your core role. Do not underestimate the amount of hard knowledge and skills that most modern jobs require. People expect you to be able to do your job!

Many roles require a high degree of technical mastery or functional expertise. However, as we progress in our organizations, we should take pride in our craft and take every opportunity to increase our knowledge, expertise, and connectedness to functional peers in other organizations. In today's ultraspecialized world, even the most general of managers must understand how the company's products work, what customers value in the products, and what innovations and technology solutions will change the business. They also need to know how to adapt to tools like artificial intelligence that will soon impact every industry business process and customer on the planet. You don't stop being a marketer just because you've become the chief marketing officer! Incompetence or ignorance is not a recipe for success.

However, people often spend too much time building these skills, missing out on developing the soft skills that have been proven to lead to a successful career. That is the gap this chapter is aiming to help fill: if not to provide all the answers, at least show the right strategies to adopt and the right approaches to pursue.

KEY ATTRIBUTES FOR SUCCESS

Over my career, I have seen many attributes that organizations of all shapes and sizes universally value. Inevitably there are organizational variants, especially in small companies. Many organizations value some of these attributes more highly than others. This is where you need to tune in to the unique environment of your organization.

In synthesizing these attributes, I have identified the fifteen that appear most valuable, and they fall into three broad groups:

- four thinking behaviors
- seven attitudinal behaviors
- four action behaviors

All these behaviors are vital to success.

THINKING BEHAVIORS

1. **Cultivating planning skills.** By now, you know I'm a huge believer in the value of planning. Love it or hate it, planning beats jumping in with both feet, and it always saves time later. And across organizations, planning helps drive alignment. I've witnessed this many times. When an executive has to pick between two people for a critical role, he or she nearly always chooses the better planner. This is partly because people who take the time to plan are more ready and able to explain their ideas, and they sound like they know more. I love the old mnemonic: PPPPP - prior preparation prevents poor performance.
2. **Creating with passion but persuading with numbers.** I learned this from a senior leader, who was referring to

how most of us plan things: with passion. We love our ideas and know why they're the right ones. But we often forget to add a vital ingredient: facts and data. Always remember: In business, passion is not enough. In business, you persuade with numbers and facts.

3. **Prioritizing.** I once had to present a plan to a senior manager. I had settled on seven priorities for the plan. Even before I started to talk through them, she interrupted me: "Efrain, I am concerned." When I asked why, she replied, "You are clearly not focused. Having a list of seven priorities tells me immediately." Differentiate between work you must do, work you should do, and work it would be nice if you did. When people have ten items on their priority lists, like the senior executive told me, it's clear the lists haven't been prioritized. If you want someone to focus on what matters, you must understand what matters most. The 80/20 rule applies here: 20 percent of the effort will yield 80 percent of the result, and to accomplish that, you have to know what's most important.

4. **Having a profit-and-loss and balance-sheet orientation.** Never lose sight of the purpose of your business. Think about this more broadly—keep the balance sheet in mind. This means if a strategy to sell more requires you to build a lot of inventory or put a lot of cash at risk, then you probably need to rethink. Just planning to sell more is not enough. How much capital are you putting at risk to sell more? Is it worth it? Is it too risky? We need to always think more broadly; it's about not only outputs but the inputs required.

ATTITUDINAL BEHAVIORS

5. **Showing a results orientation.** This is a little broader than the profits and losses. Whatever the task, focus on results more than the work involved in achieving them. Outcome-based

metrics beat activity-based metrics every time. Don't be the person who talks about how much work you did. Be the person who talks about how much you achieved.

6. **Demonstrating accountability.** This applies not only to what you have been asked to do but to what you can influence. In his book *Good to Great*, Jim Collins talks about how different types of people react when something doesn't go well: some look in the mirror, and others look at the window, pointing at other people for their explanation.[37] In the long run, mirror people do better than window people every time. They first look at what they can do before talking about what others should do.

7. **Having a bias for action.** Be proactive and look for opportunities to have an impact. Don't wait until you are told what to do. Volunteer. Raise your hand. Business is a team sport.

8. **Practicing self-management.** Managers appreciate people who don't need hand-holding. Ask for objectives and direction from leadership, not the means to achieve what you're setting out to do. You will be appreciated much more if you need less guidance to achieve the stated goals. You don't want to be consuming the bandwidth of your manager. This doesn't mean you go rogue and don't tell your manager what you are doing. If you plan (see number 1) and share your plan, your manager can give you feedback, and then you go and execute.

9. **Embracing teamwork.** Organizations, especially large ones, only succeed through collective effort. Your contribution matters little if it isn't integrated into a broader effort. People who get ahead without teamwork eventually get found out. The best me-of-tomorrow approach is to be a team player.

10. **Focusing on the solution.** People who think about solutions rather than problems are more effective. When

---

[37] James C. Collins, *Good to Great: Why Some Companies Make the Leap—and Others Don't* (New York: HarperBusiness, 2001).

presenting a problem, spend one minute talking about the problem and nine minutes talking about how you are going to solve it. Overemphasizing the problem makes some people come across as defensive, which is never good.

11. **Being a kingmaker.** This is not considered common wisdom. Share all praise for good work with the rightful owners. If you gain a reputation for giving credit to the ones who deserve it, people will offer you help when you need it. If someone helps you develop a slide and you get praise, don't eat the praise. Tell people that you were helped. Why? Next time you need help, people will be ready to help because you share the recognition.

ACTION BEHAVIORS

12. **Driving for alignment and open communications.** Always let other stakeholders in your work know what you're planning. Approach apparent conflicts with an open mind. It's better to find out early if someone is working on a project similar to yours. You don't want to duplicate work, because that means wasting money.
13. **Leveraging others.** Don't just do something because you think you can do it better than someone else. Try to avoid duplicating functions—it's a poor use of resources. I had a manager who used to tell me, "Efrain, everyone works for you; they just don't know it. Go and leverage the organization."
14. **Possessing a strong work ethic.** While hard work doesn't guarantee success, it generates respect and credibility. Of course, working hard doesn't necessarily mean hours in the office glued to your desk. But companies value employees who demonstrate a commitment to the cause, as well as resilience in the face of obstacles.

15. **Being vocal.** Don't be afraid to put your ideas forward. If you hold back for fear of being knocked down, you are shortchanging the organization of the brainpower it hired.

BEING EFFECTIVE

Even if you live these values and practices, you still might be feeling stymied in your career progression. Perhaps you think your efforts are going unnoticed, not helping you progress. One reason for this might be the need to understand the unique rules of your organization.

Just like countries have unique cultures (although that is becoming less significant in today's integrated world), companies have them too. Organizations also have commandments that we disobey at our peril.

We discussed that the surest way to increase your influence in any organization is to add value to the highest degree possible. However, certain behaviors can get you closer to this in some companies than others. And if you undermine certain fundamental organizational principles, adding value becomes more difficult.

You can also raise your level of effectiveness in any organization without making work the only thing you do in life. For most of us, a world of constant work isn't much fun. I believe that having a balanced life—managing your string, as I discussed in chapter 2—makes you more effective and productive. It keeps you energized, creative, and positive. So what is the trick? Well, I divide the effort to increase the effectiveness into three phases: (1) observation, (2) inventory, and (3) living.

PHASE 1: OBSERVATION

You can identify which behaviors your organization values through careful observation. This means opening your eyes wide, understanding what is genuinely appreciated in your workplace, and seeing how successful people behave.

The first step is to understand the *company commandments*. Every organization has commandments, either explicit or implicit, that they live by. These commandments drive the organization's culture. The greatest rewards and promotions accrue to those who act on them. But not every organization has the same commandments.

One of my favorite examples is Amazon. Although I haven't worked there, I have friends who do, and they tell me their commandments are very much lived. They call them their *management principles*, and they are well publicized within the organization. They include my favorite: "Have a backbone; disagree and commit." Their website states, "Leaders are obligated to respectfully challenge decisions when they disagree, even when doing so is uncomfortable or exhausting. Leaders have conviction and are tenacious. They do not compromise for the sake of social cohesion. Once a decision is determined, they commit wholly."

I have worked in organizations where even after a decision is made, people will say, "I am doing this, but I don't agree." Or they actively undermine the decision, sometimes working behind the scenes to frustrate it. Such behavior is not appreciated at Amazon.

It's essential to analyze behaviors carefully because there is often more to behavior than meets the eye. For example, if someone forthright and aggressive seems to do well, don't take that behavior in isolation. Sometimes people think they are exhibiting the behaviors that align with these values—obeying the commandments—but on closer observation, one realizes that they are not. I've found that understanding the company's values can be difficult.

One way that may help in some instances is to use one-on-one meetings with your manager to ask, "What values are most appreciated by the organization?" Soon after that, you can ask, "How am I exhibiting or not exhibiting such behavior?" It takes courage, but I always like to know where I stand.

PHASE 2: INVENTORY

This inventory phase is challenging. It requires you to think critically because behavior is often situation specific. To make things harder, people are frequently not told that their behavior conflicts with the organization's values. Colleagues often remain silent, which complicates things, as feedback is one of the best ways to observe and inventory desirable behaviors. The failure to understand may lead to people making the same mistakes over and over again. In the worst case, transgressors can become labeled, and their behaviors or attitudes get in the way of their advancement. All the time, they remain blissfully unaware of the reasons.

Inventorying the organization's values requires sitting down, logging those values, and ranking them. You may want to develop a list of ten to fifteen items and build a table with the names of people you consider successful in each column. You will then see which of the behaviors are present more often than not. It can also help to have someone you can compare notes with and ask questions.

The only caveat here is that some people can occasionally get confused and copy the wrong behavior. I worked with a manager who was very hierarchical with her team. She was copying a behavior from an executive she liked who also seemed hierarchical, as she thought that behavior was the executive's key success factor. In reality, it wasn't.

The other executive was indeed hierarchical, but there was so much more to her approach. She was direct, got things done, and had subject matter expertise. The manager didn't garner her team's respect, because they didn't like her management style, and unlike the executive she so admired, she had no other compensating qualities that demanded respect. She failed to retain her top performers, and people abandoned her. Her harsh style resulted in her losing her managerial status and becoming an individual contributor. She had copied the wrong behavior. She had failed to place that hierarchical attribute into a broader perspective.

PHASE 3: LIVING

Once you have observed and inventoried the organizational commandments, the next step is to demonstrate them through action. Once you understand the values that matter in your organization, then you need to live them every day. If your manager or senior executives have expressed them, you have the formula.

This means exemplifying these values. Living new values is difficult because we all have an innate resistance to change—most of us are set in our ways. This makes the path to increased effectiveness necessary but demanding. But it's tremendously helpful to have this deep awareness, based on careful analysis, showing what behaviors and attitudes are required for success.

EXERCISES TO REFOCUS YOUR CAREER

We have looked at the keys to building influence and explored the behaviors that most organizations value. I mentioned the uniqueness of individual companies and how to observe, inventory, and live those values too. However, most of us, however successful, have hit roadblocks at different times in our careers. Sometimes, we just feel stuck in a rut. Maybe we think we're doing the right thinking, displaying the right attitudes, and demonstrating the right actions. Still, our careers just aren't moving forward.

CAREER ROADBLOCKS

There are likely myriad reasons for getting stuck in this rut. We may feel stalled because of external circumstances, such as the following:

- The company is struggling strategically.
- The management chain is conservative and not forward thinking.
- Other opportunities are not opening up across the business.

However, even if the external circumstances seem healthy and the company is growing, some of us still have that feeling that other colleagues are getting better opportunities and more exciting assignments.

Throughout my career, I have known many people who worked hard, displayed the right behaviors, had the right attitude, and seemed comfortable with the company's culture and expectations but who never advanced to a level their skills and efforts promised. Equal efforts don't always result in equal rewards. Quite often, people struggle to find what I call *the right formula for success.*

At times like these, we often flail around to assign blame. Most often, we are looking for explanations in the wrong places. If you get frustrated like this, remind yourself of a few important realities:

- Every once in a while, people who don't seem as good as others in similar roles sometimes will get promoted to lead.
- If we're not one of the chosen ones, we tend to dismiss senior management as stupid. Maybe we think the successful person kissed up to senior leadership more or was a better politician.
- Promotions and assignments are not always random, down to good or bad fortune. There's often more to an assignment than meets the eye.

This is not to say that managers never make mistakes! Sometimes, utterly undeserving people get lucky breaks. However, this should never be our first assumption. I have always found it more productive to try to understand *why* things happen the way they do.

To help you plan your career and overcome some of those roadblocks, I've developed the following exercises. This will give you clarity and assist you in refocusing your efforts and continuing to advance your career in a positive direction. The goal is to help you understand how to be increasingly valued by your organization in a way that yields positions of increasing interest and responsibility. Besides, it may help you understand why things happen the way they do.

Step 1
Start with a list of attributes you have identified as the most important to help you build influence in your organization. This could be my fifteen plus two to three others unique to your organization, or it could be a subset of all of these.
Step 2
Conduct an initial self-assessment using scale points (e.g., 1–5 or 1–10) to rate your performance on these attributes. Assess honestly, with examples, of how you are demonstrating the skills or failing to. Are you leveraging the navigational tools to build a more valuable Me @ Work? What examples are there of your collaboration, resource leverage, results orientation, and so forth? Are there examples of increasing influence?
Step 3
Select three to four close colleagues and your direct manager—people you work with regularly. Send a feedback request to each of them, asking for their scores. Request comments and examples.
Step 4
Compare assessments. Average the scores from your colleagues, but I recommend weighting your manager's score more highly (that's a judgment call, depending on the degree to which your direct line manager influences your career). Look for the largest gaps between the weighted average and your own self-assessment. Build an action plan to improve your performance and close the gap on the three attributes with the largest gaps.

> **Step 5**
>
> Repeat the exercise every six to nine months.

These exercises are all about self-awareness, focus, and vision. Don't let day-to-day business challenges distract you from mastering these soft skills and becoming more valuable at work.

CHECK YOUR MOTIVATION

One final word of advice. It sounds simple, but how often do you think about *why* you get up in the morning and go to work? This exercise analyzes what motivates people *at work* and, more important, gets to a clear understanding of what motivates them in general.

The reason that I emphasize *at work* is that I first got interested in this area more than twenty years ago in a seminar in Houston, Texas. My key takeaway from the seminar was that there are five distinct motivations for people in professional environments, especially in large organizations. All of us are motivated to a greater or lesser degree by the same five factors. There are complex submotivations for sure, but in simple terms, these are the five big factors that affect us all. Of course, even though we are all motivated by these same factors, each factor's relative weight and the factors' order of importance differ for every one of us.

My opportunity to see this model in action came quickly after this seminar. I was conducting annual performance reviews for members of my team. A product manager on my team said to me, "Efrain, this year, it is OK with me if you don't give me a raise." I was a bit taken aback because, every year, one of the goals of the performance-review process is to give salary increases.

He continued, "What would be more valuable to me is if you give me the window office that became available when someone moved."

It dawned on me that money wasn't the only motivator.

Because understanding our motivation is powerful, I now make it a practice to ask all new employees or interview candidates their degree of motivation in each area, providing them with all five so that it's really a choose-the-best-answer kind of question. I will discuss later how a combination of a few of these may result in a career that, while fulfilling, may not advance much. Here are the five big factors:

1. Money: the obvious one that we all think about, to a greater or lesser degree. One truism that recent motivational research reveals is that many people are not nearly as motivated by money as they are by other factors. They often think or even say they're motivated by money, but once they reflect on it, they realize that's not their primary motivation at all. After all, why do people who haven't had a raise for years continue to work at the same company—in some cases, quite happily? We all know people like this: they are underpaid but don't leave the company. And management knows why—for many people, while money is essential, other factors just have more weight.
2. Title or rank: another somewhat visible one. We have all worked with individuals for whom title is everything. They're not hard to spot—just look at their email signatures. They're so proud of their titles that they display them in emails and PowerPoint presentations. All their neighbors know their titles. When they go out socially and meet someone new, they quickly ask, "What do you do?" We will discuss this further when we talk about value systems, but some people are highly motivated by title and rank because they feel a certain title will make others respect them more. In short, the title makes them who they are.
3. Recognition by others: seeking approval from the organization, peers, or managers. You have likely heard people say that "as long as the company recognizes my work, they don't need to promote me or pay me more money."

Such people's motivation is to receive validation from others regarding the value they provide to the organization. They want to be appreciated.
4. Achievement: how we feel internally about the work we do—much different from the other factors, which of course have more to do with how the external forces react to what we do. This motivation is about getting things done and feeling good about the accomplished work, whether someone acknowledges it or not. People motivated by achievement set their own bar and measure their results against that bar. They couldn't care less about receiving others' recognition, making more money, or getting a promotion. What matters and what drives these kinds of people is a pure feeling of achievement.
5. Environment: the motivating factor with the highest external component. This factor is about where we work, what the building looks like, how well we like our colleagues, our office's size, whether we have a window nearby, and the like. I have worked with people for whom this is the single most important motivator of all. A colleague once told me that it was OK if she didn't receive a raise, as long as she could have the next available office with a window. This aspect was clearly important to the previously mentioned product manager on my team.

Understanding your own motivation is extremely powerful. It's the starting point for moving your career in the right direction. When I say "right direction," that doesn't always mean an upward trajectory. Some people are pleased with where they are, but their frustration comes from not understanding their motivation correctly. For example, if you feel your career hasn't moved for a long time despite knowing you are hardworking, productive, and valuable to your organization, why don't you get ahead?

And when you think about it, do you feel so bad about it? It could be that on reflection, you realize your top three motivators are achievement, recognition from others, and the environment. So if you're operating within a great team, doing great work, and being recognized by your boss, you may not need that promotion or raise.

Of course, most of us to some degree or another are concerned with title and money, insofar as our livelihoods depend on a steady and sufficient income. Still, if for you these motivators are a distant fourth and fifth, you may find yourself not moving up in your organization and not feeling too poorly about it. I've known many people across organizations that fall into this category. That's why they keep coming to work and are well motivated and highly productive.

One reason I believe that organizations are triangular—fewest number of people at the top and most at the bottom—is that many people are motivated not by rank or title but by recognition, achievement, and environment. Other theories of human motivation, like self-determination theory, also support the view that money, title, and rank are not as critical as we used to think. These theories suggest that in the workplace, people value their autonomy (environment), relatedness to others (recognition), and competence (achievement).

If, on the other hand, money and title are big motivators for you, I firmly believe that the best route for you to develop your career is to avoid chasing a title or a promotion. Instead, pursue the *level of influence* you have over your organization. The more influence you have in your organization, the quicker you will get a higher title, a position of increased responsibility, and the resulting financial incentives that come with both.

CONCLUSION

Our working lives are long, and our careers are varied. Few people I know ever took a shooting star path to the top; some of the most successful people languished for years in what looked like unproductive or unsuitable roles.

Sometimes this was a matter of choice: they had contextualized their work lives. They focused on priorities and the other four mes of their lives. Occasionally they observed, inventoried, and gradually adapted their habits and practices before embarking fully on upward career mobility.

Many people I know had what looked like steady progress toward roles of increasing responsibility. In reality, there is no such thing as a smooth, uninterrupted career path; a successful career requires patience, diligence, and perseverance. As Confucius supposedly said, "It does not matter how slowly you go as long as you do not stop."

In this chapter, I covered a lot of ground and offered quite a few ideas. Hopefully, these will help you evaluate your career and identify and build the soft skills to elevate your career.

My success formula is simple:

- Focus on soft skills as much as hard skills.
- Pursue influence, not rank.
- Remember that your goal is to seek relevance and increase your value to the organization overall.
- Work is only one aspect of life. It is an important one but not the only one, and it will require different amounts of string along your life.

And, as many people smarter than I have said before, "Opportunities don't happen—you create them."

CHAPTER 6

YOUR WEALTH OF TOMORROW

There is a gigantic difference between earning a great deal of money and being rich.

—MARLENE DIETRICH

SOMEDAY ...

There are few things more challenging in life than getting a proper perspective on money. Money is unique in our modern world. It's almost impossible not to focus on it, desire it, strive for it, and spend it.

One of the most common life goals people say they have is becoming "wealthy." It's also one most of us think we will achieve. In a 2019 survey for MagnifyMoney, two-thirds of millennials and half of Gen Xers said they'd become wealthy "someday." Of course, what people mean by *wealthy* and when they think that *someday* will come differ vastly from person to person.

This notion that wealth will magically come our way often gets in the way of achieving it. We all hear the raging political debate about inequality. Still, for some reason, we have an optimistic assumption we'll end up on the right side of the wealth gap—even while the median net worth of millennial households (the middle point where half of households are more and half are less) is only $12,500.[38]

Optimism about one's financial prospects is laudable, and striving for financial success—assuming it doesn't take over our lives—is often a worthwhile endeavor. But there are some flaws to this thinking.

ADVICE FOR EVERYONE!

Money is a big subject that consumes an awful lot of time and energy. It often defines life choices, careers, friendships, where we live, and how we spend our time. It's also a topic about which there's no shortage of advice.

Reflecting on my own perspective on money, I have a confession: I find it a pretty interesting topic. It's something I've been reading about, talking about, and thinking about since I started my business career and met people who appeared to be financially comfortable, unlike me at the time. Despite this, the first lesson I remember receiving on the topic of money and savings was from Rolando, the father of my friend Sandra. Rolando always took time to get to know the kids around his daughters, and I found conversations with him enjoyable.

One day, he told me, "Efrain, when you start working, take a quarter out of every dollar you make and save it. If you can't save a quarter, save a dime, but make sure you save. It's the only way to have money for later, when you need it."

For many reasons, I wasn't able to do what he said when I first started working, but the thought stuck with me forever, and since then, I have conveyed the same idea to my children.

Managing money is the world's biggest business. The financial website Investopedia currently estimates $75 trillion of assets under

---

[38] https://www.pewsocialtrends.org/essay/millennial-life-how-young-adulthood-today-compares-with-prior-generations/.

management worldwide, just under half of which belongs to small organizations and individuals. For perspective, the annual gross domestic product of the entire US economy was $21.4 trillion in 2019.

Almost every personal finance site you view has its own list of financial-advice books. You could spend your whole life reading books about money and investing—sometimes it feels like I have! In 2018, the European professional service marketplace Consultants 500 made a list-of-lists analysis of personal-finance book recommendations. Apparently, their initial Amazon search of personal-finance books yielded sixty thousand! From lists created by top financial publications, they distilled them into a top twenty most-recommended list.[39]

As I scrolled through this list, I realized several books—especially those dealing with the psychology of money rather than the technicalities of investment strategy—were in my Audible and Kindle libraries. My point is this: there are as many opinions on how to get rich as there are financial advisers. After all, don't we need a few to handle that $75 trillion sloshing around the world?

This chapter will not present yet another novel investment strategy. I'm tempted to say that's because there's nothing new under the sun, but the more pertinent reason is that I'm not a financial adviser. I'm not here to help you get rich quick. But if you've read up to here, you understand I like practical shortcuts—filters to help sift through duplicative or irrelevant advice and find nuggets sitting in the bottom of the gold pan. This chapter offers a few nuggets not just from books I've read or financial advice gurus I've talked to but also from the school of hard knocks. It's not a substitute for a cute investment strategy or a stock tip from your favorite aunt, but it will help demystify your relationship with money. Then you can pick and choose from this cacophony of advice and have the kind of relationship with money that will benefit that me of tomorrow.

---

[39] https://www.blog.consultants500.com/accounting-audit-advisory/top-20-best-finance-books-recommended-times-finance-pros/.

WEALTH AND INCOME

WHAT DO WE MEAN BY WEALTH?

The first issue we need to tackle is, What is wealth? One startling takeaway from the survey I referenced earlier is how diverse people's ideas of what it means to be wealthy are. Most people define wealth vaguely as being able to live comfortably without worrying about their finances.

That in itself is problematic—I know plenty of wealthy people who fret about nothing else. Score keeping among the superrich is legendary. They battle for places on *Fortune* lists of the wealthiest individuals. Even in today's troubled times, there was quite a bit of chatter when Mr. Bezos's little company hit a $1 trillion market capitalization. As of December 2020, it was worth more than $1.6 trillion! For perspective, mathematicians estimate that were it possible to stack one trillion dollar bills, they would reach 67,688 miles, more than a quarter of the distance from the earth to the moon. Laid side by side on the ground, the bills would cover 3,992 square miles, twice the size of Delaware.[40] This is staggering and once again makes the debate rage about the morality of wealth. Bezos owns 11.1 percent of this incredible sum.[41] That's a discussion for another day.

At the other end of the scale, one in five millennials specified that being wealthy means having at least $500,000. According to the Federal Reserve's 2016 Survey of Consumer Finances, this is actually lower than the average US household net worth, $692,000.

However, this is a dramatically skewed picture because it includes superwealthy individuals. A better measure is the median (midpoint) of $97,300. For those aged under thirty-five, this falls to $11,100. Many of us are striving for a wealth point that's relatively modest and,

---

[40] https://www.ehd.org/science_technology_largenumbers.php.
[41] https://www.investopedia.com/articles/insights/052816/top-4-amazon-shareholders-amzn.asp.

in reality, far lower than the amount that could buy even an average home in many US coastal cities.

Another inconvenient truth is that many people view wealth in a completely different way. Instead of an absolute amount of savings or assets, they see wealth as tied to their incomes, the type of jobs they hold, or their professions—in other words, their *potential* wealth rather than their actual wealth. Having a well-paid job or excellent future income prospects makes you *feel* wealthy, as your bank balance is frequently replenished, but you shouldn't confuse this feeling with actual wealth. This is one of the most common and most dangerous mistakes people make when thinking about their personal finances.

ASSESSING YOUR WEALTH

There's another simple way of assessing your wealth that I have found more useful. Of course, you could calculate how much your house is worth, how many loans you have, and what you could sell your car for. That kind of calculation is fine, but there are often many unknown variables. Any asset's value is only what it will fetch when sold, and it's hard to price some illiquid assets. My method is simple and actionable. Your comfortable job, career, or house may not be the financial ace in the hole you think it is if values and economic orthodoxy are turned upside down.

The following exercise will help. I based it on many conversations I had with my friend Roberto, who has similar views.

1. Imagine that all your income sources dry up tomorrow. That means no more paychecks, no more interest or dividends from your bank or investments, no check from the person renting your spare room, and so forth. You have nothing coming in.
2. Estimate your typical monthly bills: mortgage, rent, car payment, utilities, medical bills, school loans, credit card bills, and so on. If you know this from your budget, so much the

better, but sadly, many people don't know what a budget is. According to statistics compiled by the site Debt.com, only one in three Americans maintains a household budget. Only 30 percent have a long-term financial plan. This third of us are much more likely to be people making more than $75,000 per year. Astonishingly, according to website Calendar, the average American schedules fewer than four and a half hours *per year* on his or her calendar for finances. These budget issues compose a whole area of financial insanity. Very simply, without a budget, you have no control or understanding of your money at all. However, leaving that aside, for this simple test, make an estimate. Be current and realistic. Don't think about all the corners you could cut and the meals out you could forgo if this worst-case money drought were to happen.

3. Finally, assess how many months or years you could survive without stress with this same budget, realistically, on the money you have in your bank or savings. Just divide your available cash by your realistic current monthly budget. Place yourself on the following scale (figure 11):

LEVEL 1

You have nothing in reserve. If your car breaks down, or your windshield is shattered, there's no spare money to fix it. If income ended tomorrow, bills would just accumulate. In other words, your expenses are equal to your income, and you have no rainy-day fund.

LEVEL 2

You have some emergency savings. You could pay for emergency plumbing repair, a roof leak, or an air-conditioning problem. You could take a trip across the country for a family emergency without dumping the expense on the never-never of a credit card bill. You could forgo your next paycheck, or even your next two or three.

LEVEL 3

Now you have a few months' money in the bank. If you lose your job tomorrow, there's time to find another one. A health setback won't cause you an additional financial headache. You can deal with other problems without adding more stress from your bank balance or escalating credit card debt. You have breathing space.

LEVEL 4

You could go for a year or two without working. You can lose our job and be truly selective as to what you want to do; you could go back to school or take a different career direction without getting stressed out. You have the space and time to think about your life, your goals and other elements of your happiness.

LEVEL 5

You don't need to work again because your savings produce enough income to cover all your expenses. Your financial needs are covered.

Figure 11.

So what's your score? Are you at level 4 or level 5? Can you afford to relax with no financial stress? Can you count your money and manage your investments with a detached academic interest?

Just as vital, are you at the level you want to be? Or are you one of those many people whose financial future depends on gifts or loans from family and friends? An anticipated inheritance?

These are all possible sources of future wealth. After all, the landmark 2017 academic study by French economist Thomas Piketty and his colleagues showed that approximately 60 percent of all US wealth is inherited.[42] But this doesn't measure your *current* wealth, and it doesn't help you make the changes to your financial habits that will increase your wealth score over time. This exercise assesses your actual wealth right now, not a mythical time when all sorts of theoretical sources of new money have come in.

INCOME VERSUS WEALTH

Wealth is a simple concept. The preceding exercise takes a simple snapshot and assesses your practical financial resources. This assessment is independent of the job you hold, the prospects you have, the possible appreciation of the house you own, and the expectation of loans and gifts from friends and family.

But let's talk about the dynamics of wealth—how it changes and how you can make it change. Even if you're at level 4 or 5, your wealth will decrease if all your income stops tomorrow, as you'll be spending more than you have coming in. Even if you're at level 1 or 2, your wealth will grow if you bring in more than you spend. English writer Charles Dickens put it more elegantly: "Annual income twenty pounds, annual expenditure nineteen [pounds] nineteen [shillings] and six [pence], result happiness. Annual income twenty pounds, annual expenditure twenty pounds, nought and six, result misery."

Of course, you might say it's easier to achieve Dickens's happy

---

[42] Facundo Alvaredo, Bertrand Garbinti, and Thomas Piketty, "On the Share of Inheritance in Aggregate Wealth: Europe and the USA, 1900–2010."

state if you're making more money. But here's the important part: your level of income is only one part of the equation. Increasing rather than decreasing wealth is not just about making a higher income, although that's always nice. It's *how* you manage what you have coming in and accumulating wealth. The reason we get ourselves into financial trouble, why we find ourselves at wealth level 1 rather than wealth level 5, is often not because we don't have enough income but because we do not understand Dickens's simple formula for happiness.

One day, early in my career, as a newly minted executive at a Fortune 50 company, I received my first invitation to a divisional off-site business review. To me, this was a big deal. Our division head held these events every quarter to huddle with her senior team and strategize. I was mixing with the movers and shakers, moving into the political environment that I talked about in chapter 5. The event was at a beautiful hotel on a lake, about forty-five minutes from home. I carpooled to the event with a colleague, someone well within the inner circle, who lived close by. The venue had a separate parking area next to the lake. When we arrived, I couldn't help noticing that almost every car in the parking lot was a late-model European vehicle. There were BMWs, Mercedes-Benzes, and more than a few Porsches. My friend and I had a great relationship and liked to kid around with each other, and I saw just the opportunity to do it.

I turned to my colleague and said, "See all these cars? Why are we showing up in your Honda Civic?"

He smiled. "Want to get a brokerage statement from any of those fancy-car drivers and compare it to mine?"

Although he never showed me that brokerage account, his response crystallized something in my mind: physical assets don't necessarily correlate to wealth. That insight started my reading from one of those lists I mentioned. I particularly liked *The Millionaire Next Door* by Stanley and Danko and *The Happiness Hypothesis* by Jonathan

Haidt.[43] Stanley and Danko show that the car you drive or the size of your house doesn't explain wealth. Haidt teaches how human beings chase money as a way to happiness. Though money is necessary, it does not buy happiness. More on that later.

My car pool friend was a respected leader at the company. But his colleagues were always taking verbal jabs at him for his Honda Civic. It became quite the running joke at executive get-togethers. Later in my career, I became the object of similar jokes for my vehicle choice; in fact, some colleagues were severely critical. One BMW-driving colleague told me it was inappropriate for a company director to drive an old-model Japanese car. I was very much in the minority.

Of course, I couldn't have cared less, but this kind of talk can affect other junior executives rising up the ranks. It crystallizes and reinforces the perception that a particular title and status at work require a certain image—certain brands of clothing, shoes, cars, cell phones, and so on. It's as if, like with medieval nobles, our status requires ostentatious displays of luxury to impress others. Of course, being smart, clean, and well presented is essential, especially in roles like sales. I'm not advocating sloppiness or lack of seriousness. Still, in my experience, overt ostentation doesn't always play well with either customers or colleagues. It may communicate apparent success, but experienced people see through superficial displays. And customers may worry that you are charging too much if you can afford such finery. There's no rule that having a certain title means you have to drive a particular car or wear a specific watch brand. That kind of attitude is for those who don't know the difference between income and wealth.

Another important lesson came when a friend of mine was laid off quite early in both of our careers. He called and told me two things: first, how stressed he was with his new baby and stay-at-home

---

[43] Thomas J. Stanley and William D. Danko, *The Millionaire Next Door: The Surprising Secrets of America's Wealthy*, 25th anniversary ed. (Lanham: Taylor Trade Publishing, 2016); Jonathan Haidt, *The Happiness Hypothesis: Finding Modern Truth in Ancient Wisdom* (New York: Basic Books, 2006).

wife and, second, that his neighbor three houses down had also gotten laid off but was oddly cool, calm, and collected about it.

Unlike my friend, his neighbor understood the difference between income and wealth. He measured his wealth not in absolute dollars but in the number of months he could be out of work without it impacting his lifestyle. He was at level 3, while my friend was somewhere between levels 1 and 2. The simple lesson is this: never confuse income and wealth.

INCOME AND SPENDING

Another problem with our tendency to equate income with wealth is that it drives showy spending. We do well, earn promotions, get bonuses or boosts in our pay grades, start mixing with the inner circles of our companies, and lose our sense of proportion. Our careers may be on a roll, and suddenly, we begin to act the part. Naturally, we're proud of what we've accomplished, but we think that our success means our trajectories will continue on the same smooth upward path.

In business, this is never the case. Companies restructure, leaders come and go, products get dropped, and sometimes technological change drives out whole staff layers or makes seemingly secure professions obsolete. It's unlikely you will escape unscathed throughout your entire career. Be happy when times are good, but be prepared when they are not. Become the ruler of your money, and don't rely on an increasing income to sustain your lifestyle. As the Filipino proverb says, "If you make a habit of buying things you do not need, you will soon be selling things you do."

THE DIDEROT EFFECT

The Diderot effect is a well-observed social phenomenon whereby people end up buying things they don't really need. The term was coined by the Canadian anthropologist Grant McCracken, who named it for the eighteenth-century French philosopher Denis Diderot. Simply put, spending becomes cumulative because one purchase makes others psychologically necessary.

The concept is that if you acquire something that's out of sync with your other possessions, you are driven to change these other possessions to match the new purchase. In Diderot's case, he received a scarlet dressing gown as a gift. Because it was such a beautiful and elegant garment, he felt the rest of his wardrobe and furnishings were insufficient to match this new gown. To paraphrase McCracken, they were not culturally complementary. Consequently, Diderot went on a spending spree, racking up huge debts to buy items that matched his new gown's elegance. As James Clear, author of *Atomic Habits*, observed when discussing this effect, "Life has a natural tendency to become filled with more. We rarely look to downgrade, to simplify, to eliminate, to reduce. Our natural inclination is always to accumulate, add, upgrade, and build upon."[44]

We are all like Diderot, to a greater or lesser degree. When we buy new cell phones, how often do we then gather accompanying accoutrements—cases, car chargers, headphones, and so forth—to match our original purchases? Or perhaps a new outfit or dress generates a need for shoes, purses, and jewelry? These may seem like small additions and, in the case of the dress, perhaps necessary ones.

This effect also applies across categories and may result in new cars, furniture, and even houses. It applies to many of my BMW-driving, expensive-watch-wearing colleagues at that executive meeting at the lake. Their increased incomes and statuses drove their new luxury-car purchases, and they added other fancy accompaniments as cultural complements. This effect is quite insidious. It can quickly drive us to spend more of our incomes than we need to and lead even apparently well-heeled executives into a level 1 or 2 wealth trap.

James Clear recommends reducing exposure, only buying items

---

[44] James Clear, *Atomic Habits: Tiny Changes, Remarkable Results—an Easy and Proven Way to Build Good Habits and Break Bad Ones* (New York: Avery, 2018); James Clear, https://jamesclear.com/diderot-effect.

that fit your current system, setting limits, giving away an old item for a new one, delaying new purchases, and just letting go of desires. However, the first step in combatting this phenomenon is recognizing it and understanding how it can quickly drive us down the wealth scale.

COMMITMENT EXPENSES

There's another dimension to consider. Not all expenses are the same. The Diderot effect is a psychological trigger for spending. Sometimes, there's a simple, practical trigger based on necessity. Some purchases, by their nature, commit you to others, occasionally long-term ones. Even if the initial purchase doesn't make you happy, you're committed anyway.

If you buy an expensive house, it comes with necessary baggage: higher energy expenses for heating or air-conditioning; maintenance costs for the pool; and extra gardening, equipment, and lawn treatments for all that shrubbery. The same is true for a high-end car: there will be higher service and maintenance costs, parts cost more, it uses more gas, you need to clean it more frequently, and so on. The basic idea is that once you commit to a big purchase, it can bring a long tail of expenses, many of which you might not have accounted for.

These expenses should be considered differently than, say, a Caribbean vacation or a trip to Europe. Those expenditures, while extravagant, don't come with a long tail. When the vacation is over, you can start to accumulate funds for the next adventure. But if you acquire a vehicle that consumes $500 per month, you are still under the gun for another $500 when month 2 or month 22 comes around. Crucially, it reduces your capacity to save.

Some financial advisers tell us that one way to avoid the long tail associated with big purchases is to rent what you need, not own it. Some people say they dream of buying a vacation home or owning a boat. But, actually, the dream is not about the ownership at all—it's about the feeling that the related experience brings. So the dream is not the home or the boat: it's the feeling of lying on a sandy beach or puttering off for a few peaceful hours on the open water. It's not remembering to hire someone to put up storm shutters or replace a bilge pump.

After all, how many times have you been to someone's lake house? You will find the person often has a boat or a Jet Ski, as well as a golf cart to drive around. These items weren't in the equation when he or she assessed the cost of the home.

There's precious little involved in these experiences that can't be rented rather than owned: vacation homes; fancy cars; and even high-end designer clothes, if your dream is to wear them. Most of us have neither the time nor inclination to visit that vacation home more than a couple of times a year. By renting, your only obligation is to roll up and have a great time, not having to deal with utility bills or repairs. We need to understand what the dream really is, not a version of it that commits us to more painful expenses.

THE PSYCHOLOGY OF SPENDING

In the last section, I discussed the crucial difference between income and wealth. A high level of income often drives us to spend, perhaps unnecessarily. We realize that not all expenses are equal and that sometimes high costs beget annoying recurring ones.

But there's another crucial issue that affects our whole relationship with money. That question is that thorny old chestnut, Does spending money make us happier? We need to unpack this at a personal level. Unraveling this piece of individual psychology should let us divorce the feeling of well-being that comes from increased income from the desire to buy expensive things with that income.

SPENDING AND HAPPINESS

Most of us enjoy spending money. After all, what's money for, if not to spend? Few of us have the mental discipline or cultural detachment to embrace those minimalist philosophies that question our materialistic consumer society. As a well-paid friend of mine once remarked about living in America, "It doesn't matter how much money you make—this country has a way of taking it off you."

In the 2017 *Time* magazine special edition "The Science of Happiness," writer David Futrelle referenced a famous ad when Toyota's luxury car brand Lexus was barnstorming the US: "Whoever said money can't buy happiness isn't spending it right."[45]

It's a smart play on the age-old debate. We know that money and happiness are connected; acquiring new things or having a unique experience facilitated by spending cash gives us excitement or pleasure. Sometimes we get that shot of dopamine from the simplest splurge. But how about the modern-day equivalent of Diderot's scarlet gown—a beautiful piece of clothing or maybe a shiny new cell phone? Or even something more costly, like a new car? How much happiness do these things provide?

Psychologists have been researching this question for years. Much of the recent work has focused on a related question that marketers and advertisers have been wrestling with: Do we experience greater happiness from buying material things or from buying experiences? The added complication with this question is that many material goods—like a new car, perhaps—actually deliver future experiences.

Most research supports the conclusion that we garner greater pleasure through experiences rather than things. One reason is that material acquisitions are more likely to give us buyer's remorse. Another is that it's much harder to compare different people's experiences than their different material assets. Furthermore, that initial dopamine shot from a new purchase fades over time.

However, material things *can* make us happy. It's just that they

---

[45] https://time.com/4856954/can-money-buy-you-happiness/.

often *don't*. In their fascinating book *Happy Money: The Science of Happier Spending*, professors Elizabeth Dunn and Michael Norton found seventeen thousand articles on the relationship between money and happiness.[46] Although so many of these suggest that money doesn't buy happiness, the authors set out to explore whether it can and how you can "get more happiness for your money as a consumer."

Other studies have shown that people are happier if the things they purchase match their personalities. For example, a sociable extrovert is more content spending money on a night out with friends, while an introvert is more comfortable staying in with a book.

In chasing this elusive moment of pleasure, we often spend money we can't afford. Just as we should pause to think what the me of tomorrow would thank the me of today for (see chapter 1), we should also pause and take control of our financial decisions. Think about what you do with your income, and understand it won't always be increasing exponentially.

It's always good practice to pause and question ourselves when we sense, consciously or not, that the purchase we're about to make will make us happier. It can, but very often, it doesn't. Some researchers say that when you buy a new car, you feel good for thirty days, and then you take it for granted. We get more money, buy more stuff, and then fail to think about wealth and the real goal—we forget to make decisions with the me of tomorrow in mind.

SPENDING AND SHOW

In my earlier story about the cars at the lake, my colleague drove an old Honda Civic. He lived in a modest house in a nice neighborhood. Many of his colleagues at the meeting—many of them junior and compensated less than him—drove high-end cars and lived in large houses much fancier than his, with pools and land around them.

---

[46] Elizabeth Dunn and Michael Norton, *Happy Money: The Science of Happier Spending* (2014).

People comparing the neighborhoods would automatically assume that his colleagues were wealthy, high-flying executives who had accumulated stacks of money.

The reality was very different. The simple truth that took me a while to learn is that someone's house, car, watch, or clothing is not an indicator of wealth. What you show to the world is not what you are worth. Investor Warren Buffett (net worth $73 billion) drives a 2014 Cadillac; as recently as 2013, Jeff Bezos, CEO of Amazon, drove a Honda Accord. Every person has his or her own money and happiness equation. Material things you show to the world are just reflections of what you are spending, not your wealth.

SPENDING AND EGO

Living below your means requires you to suppress your ego. People ridiculed my colleague because of his Honda Civic, and my choice of vehicle generated similar wry observations. However, as journalist, author, and venture capitalist Morgan Housel has observed, people with enduring personal-finance success tend not to give a damn what others think about them.[47] He neatly defines savings as "the gap between your ego and your income."

Admirable though this trait may be, it's not an easy trick to pull off. Never estimate the power of peer pressure. If you're a successful businessperson or on your way to becoming one, a certain level of ego and competitive pride comes with the territory. It's a hard thing to suppress. However, when you feel tugged toward that BMW dealership or real estate office, take a second and check your ego. If you go ahead and spend, make sure it's you making the decision and not your ego! Many successful executives find themselves overstretched and landing at level 1 or 2 on the wealth scale because they let their egos make spending decisions.

---

[47] https://www.cnbc.com/2020/07/06/follow-5-money-rules-while-still-young-or-regret-later-in-life-finance-expert.html.

SPENDING AND RELATIONSHIPS

As discussed in chapter 4, people with positive, productive, and close personal relationships live longer, happier lives. And one of the leading causes of relationship problems is financial stress. A 2018 survey by financial education company Ramsey Solutions listed money fights as the second leading cause of divorce, behind infidelity.[48] Other research supports that finding. Money-related conflicts are frequently cited as a reason for divorce, and couples who argue about finances at least once a week are 30 percent more likely to divorce. If couples enter marriage with no assets rather than at least $10,000, they are 70 percent more likely to divorce within three years.

Having compatible attitudes toward money is also an important consideration when choosing a long-term partner. If you and your partner don't see eye to eye on spending and saving, it's challenging to achieve harmony.

EYES ON THE PRIZE: WHAT'S THE REAL GOAL HERE?

So what is the real goal? When people tell pollsters that their goal in life is to be wealthy, what do they mean? They're probably not picturing the nursery rhyme king in his countinghouse or even the modern-day version—the person who spends every waking hour scrutinizing his or her portfolio. The real goal is much more profound. They likely don't seek wealth or even the houses, cars, and boats that wealth can buy. What they really want is freedom and independence.

In the 1987 Oliver Stone classic *Wall Street*, the villainous character Gordon Gekko, played by Michael Douglas, sums up his goal: "Rich enough not to waste time." Of course, unlike him, we're not thinking about being rich enough to have our own jets. More likely, we're picturing ourselves somewhere between levels 4 and 5 on the wealth scale. We are dreaming of a life where income doesn't

---

[48] https://www.daveramsey.com/pr/money-ruining-marriages-in-america.

dictate spending; where we can ride the waves of working life with a somewhat detached air; where, if things become intolerable at work, we can say "hasta la vista" without a second thought; where we can take the summer off to explore a different business idea or take that trip to Latin America. We are imagining a life where we can live how we want, where we want, free of the daily economic hardship that afflicts 95 percent of the world's population.

But there should be another goal too. Financial stress is a severe burden for large numbers of people. Here, I'm not referring to the homeless or the working poor, the single mom working two low-paying jobs, or the disabled veteran struggling to make ends meet. Financial stress also afflicts people with high incomes and supposedly secure jobs. A 2019 survey of more than ten thousand Americans conducted by global salary-based lender Salary Finance reveals that financial stress affects 48 percent of the US workforce. Stress is especially acute in high-cost markets.[49] Tellingly, this survey shows that financial stress is independent of income and that a high salary is a poor predictor of financial health. Forty percent of Americans earning more than $100,000 per year are financially unstable, at a 1–2 wealth level, and 25 percent of people earning more than $160,000 per annum are at level 1—that is, living paycheck to paycheck with no savings. These findings are shocking, but they match my own experience of high-flying executives and others around me too. Some of those people at the lake meeting could well have been at a 1–2 wealth level.

Like other forms of stress, financial pressures have a devastating impact on mental health. The survey showed that people with financial stress are three times more likely to suffer from anxiety and panic attacks and four times more likely to suffer from depression and suicidal thoughts. As we now know, stress is one of the most toxic ingredients in terms of our overall physical health. A lifetime of this kind of pressure might well render us unable to appreciate the benefits of finally escaping it.

---

[49] https://www.salaryfinance.com/us/.

SIMPLE MONEY TACTICS

Once we understand the downfalls and risks of poor financial management, we must take all necessary steps to ameliorate them. We can't all become personal-finance experts, and we wouldn't want to. It's unnecessary to have read all the books or absorbed all the smart investment strategies to build wealth for the me of tomorrow. I recommend just a few simple tactics. If you employ these, you will become the ruler of your money and won't allow your money to rule you.

You may have some version of these tactics in place already. There are all sorts of possible variations. The details matter less than the principle. The approach serves two essential purposes: (1) it sets you up to build wealth, and (2) it teaches you the discipline you need for financial success. Like so many other improvements in life, the secret is to build a habit. Then the behavior becomes second nature. As Charles Duhigg reminds us, the power of habit is a formidable thing indeed.[50]

SEPARATE INCOME FROM WEALTH

Earlier in the chapter, I talked about how wealth—and therefore freedom—is only partly related to income. Of course, everyone needs income of one kind or another to increase his or her wealth. But the conventional view that it's easier for people earning more money to save than it is for people earning less is simply not accurate. As discussed earlier, there are so many strong ties between income and spending that consumption often rises just as fast as, sometimes faster than, our incomes. Then we can't reduce it when income falls, which, at some point in life, it inevitably will. I have known executives making nearly a million per year at level 1 or level 2 on

---

[50] Charles Duhigg, *The Power of Habit: Why We Do What We Do in Life and Business* (New York: Random House Trade Paperbacks, 2014).

the wealth scale. Simply, their expenses, lifestyle, and requirements for extravagant consumption rise faster than their earnings.

There are even more dramatic illustrations. Think of the problems so many professional athletes run into, even with annual earnings in the multiple millions. The ESPN documentary *Broke* estimated that 78 percent of NFL players are out of money less than two years after leaving the game. There are high-profile financial casualties across a broad range of sports, from Boris Becker in tennis; to John Daly in golf; to Mike Tyson and Evander Holyfield in boxing; to former NBA champion Dennis Rodman, who apparently squandered career earnings of $27 million in less than a year.

On the flip side, I've seen people with meager incomes ascend the wealth scale. I vividly remember an incident from my college graduation. An older aunt came up to me and presented me with a very generous gift. She worked as a cashier in retail and for the city revenue office her whole life. She lived a modest life in a modest home. However, she attended every family event, took vacations to the US, and never seemed stressed about finances, unlike some of my other relatives.

Furthermore, she never talked about what she was making and what new things she was buying. Reflecting on this now, I realize that she was probably higher on the wealth scale than my executive friends with their high salaries. She understood that wealth is something we build over time. She had avoided all those traps that high income sets for us. We can all achieve this by, using Dickens's definition, choosing happiness over misery.

BECOME THE RULER, NOT THE RULED

Of course, achieving level 4 or 5 doesn't happen by accident. First, you must understand the pitfalls of competing for status and appreciate that some purchases come with unwanted financial baggage. Then you must grasp your personal connection between material things and happiness. No two people have the same equation. And of course, keep your eyes on the prize: freedom from stress and independence from jobs and income.

Remember: either you are the ruler of money—the king or queen—or it will surely rule you. My aunt was the queen of her money. Some of my highly compensated friends were its subordinates. The simple tactics will help you become the ruler, but you can't get there without the right understanding and mindset. Here are some of my suggestions.

THE FREEDOM FUND

As soon as you can, set up a fund in a separate bank account. Call it something that reflects your goal: your independence fund, your freedom fund, or even your hasta la vista fund. One of my good friends used more colorful language, prefacing the word *money* with an expletive to convey exactly what he would say to his boss if he ever wanted to quit because of poor treatment. Embody your goal in the name, and refer to it that way. As such, it will become your North Star, your guide to financial freedom.

From *any* income, from whatever source—salaries, interest, dividends, tax refunds, bonuses, gifts—take a percentage and invest in the fund. Ideally, this should be 20–25 percent, as my friend's dad advised me. Of course, when earnings are low, this might be money you desperately need. Maybe you need to start with 10–15 percent, but the discipline should always be there. You might think of it as a religious tithe.

Make that fund inviolate. Think of the fund as a lockbox, a vault. Picture those old-school fire alarms that say in large letters "Only break glass in case of fire." Only touch the fund in an absolute emergency, a life-or-death situation.

Of course, feel free to manage the fund's contents as it accumulates, but ensure you invest it conservatively, with minimal risk commensurate with acceptable returns. Today that would be a money market fund or fixed-income securities with minimal volatility.

REAL ESTATE RULES

You also need to develop the right mindset about real estate. A house is often the most significant purchase most people make during their lifetimes. Housing is also one of the most popular ways to generate additional income and build wealth. Depending on the market you choose, it can be an excellent way to drive supplementary income.

However, never underestimate the time and effort involved in making a success of a real estate business. Over the years, I've been involved in many real estate transactions, as both a buyer and a seller. It's an area of spending in which buyers repeatedly make some simple mistakes.

Most buyers get preapproved for a loan before looking at houses. The amount they are approved for often creates their purchase price ceiling. However, in my experience, too many buyers stretch this envelope. Sometimes encouraged by brokers who show them "slightly" more expensive houses, buyers get seduced by homes 10–15 percent over their ceiling. They believe that, somehow, they can "make it work." Buyers end up with houses they can't afford, trusting that that potential appreciation and their expectation of increased income will take care of the shortfall.

When they get their houses, these buyers face commitment expenses—larger mortgage payments, additional energy costs, and higher maintenance bills. These expenses reduce their wealth and drive them down the wealth scale. The added cost of living jeopardizes their freedom funds. Besides, some of their new neighbors in those wealthier neighborhoods may have tastes that tempt them to spend more. An exotic vacation, a pool, and a weekend car are just some examples.

A much smarter solution for you is to look for properties 5–10 percent below your ceiling. In this way, you can save some down payment, make any necessary improvements, or, better still, allocate more cash to the freedom fund. This caution doesn't come easily. We are so focused on the me of today and the excitement of something wonderful. But when problems arise, as they inevitably do, having a lighter financial load is always worth the sacrifice. I guarantee there are benefits of playing the long game.

Years ago, one of my friends had a huge beautiful home. After returning from the first few dinner parties at his wonderful house, I often reflected on how nice it would be to have a larger and nicer home like his. Very quickly, though, I realized I was just succumbing to me-of-today thinking. Our family didn't need a larger home. Buying a house like that would significantly impact our family savings and the college choices we could offer our children. Before long, my thinking after future dinners changed utterly. Whenever I arrived home, my first thought was *I'm so glad we don't own a large home like his.*

If you are a businessperson, you understand that carrying inventory has costs. If you are not a businessperson, do an internet search for "why carrying excess inventory is not good business practice." The net is *because unused inventory costs money.* In simple terms, why buy a year's worth of toothpaste? You are tying up money in an asset that doesn't need to be used for a while. Buying a larger home than you would ever need is the same thing. Think of a big house as carrying a large inventory. You have rooms you hardly use but that consume resources—furniture, electricity, cleaning, and so forth.

NOTES ON VEHICLES

As with houses, I've bought and sold a few vehicles over the years. And I'm not going to presume to tell you what you need or what to buy. However, there are a couple of useful ideas I keep in mind when car shopping—one obvious, the other less so.

The obvious point that most people grasp is that—rather like the Diderot effect, or the long tail of expenses—luxury brands are intrinsically more expensive to maintain. Even if the warranty for big-ticket service items may look attractive, simple services always cost more, and warranties can be invalidated if you choose the local repair shop over the high-priced dealership for your lube job. Replacement items like tires and lights usually cost more and sometimes require a dealer visit to replace them.

Less well understood is the expense trade-off between vehicle maintenance and depreciation. A new car will require lower repair costs than an older model. However, what you save in maintenance will likely be dwarfed by the value losses in vehicle depreciation. Years 1–3 of a car's life are the worst for depreciation. After that, the depreciation curve flattens. The percentage of annual loss in vehicle value is significantly less in years 3–5 or 5–7 than in years 1–3. These losses often dwarf the increased maintenance costs over the same period.

This is not to say that you should never buy new; just keep these factors in mind before you assume that shiny new vehicle is really saving you money.

PAYING FOR YOUR DREAMS

It has become an article of faith in today's society that you must follow your passion. Stories abound of world-renowned musicians, artists, chefs, athletes, and others whose single-minded dedication to their passions brought them fame and fortune. Commencement ceremonies are replete with speakers telling fresh-faced graduates that they must "follow their dreams."

I am all for enjoying what you do in life; choosing an unfulfilling career is a recipe for long-term disillusionment. However, we need to understand that achieving fame and fortune from our passions is the exception rather than the rule. I prefer the advice of comedian Chris

Rock: "You can be anything you want to be; you can be anything you're good at, as long as they're hiring."[51]

The point here is that, for most people, dreams don't come free. Many "passion" occupations, especially artistic ones, require large slices of luck, in addition to the obvious ingredients of talent and dedication, to turn them from fun into profit. Years spent in low-income, low-wealth-generating careers can create frustration and resentment. A job that earns a good income allows you to build your freedom fund and a financial platform so the me of tomorrow can pursue these passions later. Besides, once you become good at something, you may be surprised how it becomes your passion.

FREE MONEY

One of the lessons I had to learn early was how to take advantage of free money, especially as I was trying to save at least 10 percent of my salary. One of my colleagues at work, Manny, helped me understand the first one: matching dollars on the company's 401(k). This is money that is free but requires you to put money aside. Most companies that offer 401(k) have matching dollars, but employees age twenty-five and under enroll only one-third of the time in the offered 401(k), and only 16 percent take full advantage of the 401(k) match.[52]

The second idea may not be for everyone, but it may work for a few. This one comes from my having seen people use their debit cards everywhere. Debit cards are valuable in that you spend only what you have and they work like credit cards. Good. But what if you know you'd be disciplined and judicious enough to pay a credit card balance at the end every month? For those people, there are plenty of products around that give money back. You just have to watch TV one evening, and you will see a ton of commercials. If you can be

---

[51] https://www.nationalreview.com/2018/02/chris-rock-tamborine-we-need-bullies-marital-fidelity-no-pornography/.
[52] https://www.businessinsider.com/young-people-401k-2015-6.

disciplined, you should never use a debit card. You should get a card with your favorite type of reward—frequent-flier miles, cheap gas, or some such perk—and use that instead. If you are trying to save 10 percent of your salary, this can be 20 percent of it, or 2 percent of your salary! I have even seen a few with no membership fees.

"IF YOU CAN'T MEASURE IT, YOU CAN'T IMPROVE IT"

This is another one of my favorite Peter Drucker quotes. I will talk about the general importance of measuring progress in the next chapter, but it is certainly one thing I find key to developing financial health in particular. I track my finances with Quicken, and when I first introduced my son to it after he finished college, I also suggested a 9:00 a.m. review on Saturdays of what he had spent throughout the week. If you can't do this every week, every other is better than not tracking your spending at all. One of my friends who has had the most success in developing financial independence does a yearly assessment. He takes a snapshot at the beginning of the year, and he does the same at the end and compares. Note: there is no need to obsess; just give it the right amount of string as to minimize the impact that financial problems have on your other mes.

CONCLUSION

As this chapter shows, I firmly believe that you should divorce your income from your wealth. The confusion of these two concepts underpins so much financial stress and poor decision-making. Your financial goal should be to pursue independence and freedom and to eliminate the toxic stress of financial pressure from your life. Of course, reaching this goal requires understanding and discipline. You should be looking to build a freedom fund as quickly as possible. Don't spend money because of perceived status, show, or a desire to emulate others. That's not the path to wealth and independence. It is unlikely the people you want to impress will be there to help you when you get in financial trouble.

Some might view this approach as another example of sacrificing the pleasure of today for the joy of tomorrow. However, the truth is more nuanced. We all need to understand our own personal value equations between money and happiness. For example, there's nothing inherently wrong with buying a nice car if it makes you genuinely happy over and above a unique life experience. But for most people, the thrill of a new purchase is ephemeral. Building wealth and achieving financial independence as soon as possible are disciplines that will give you a better life, more freedom, and ultimately more choices. Don't be subservient to your income; instead, become the ruler of your wealth. Learn to develop financial health as soon as you can.

CHAPTER 7

REACHING TOMORROW

> The first wealth is health.
>
> —RALPH WALDO EMERSON

Having addressed financial wealth, it makes perfect sense to move to the most significant wealth of all. This book urges you to visualize the me of tomorrow. If you've read up to here, by now, you might concede that seizing the day isn't the best approach to life. While the world pressures us to maximize today's gratification, thankfully, for most of us, there will be a me of tomorrow. We should strive to make sure that those future mes tip their hats to today's me, thanking him or her for enabling a fulfilling life—balanced, educated, prosperous, financially secure.

However, to enjoy that fulfilling life, that future me must be healthy. There's little point in success, great relationships, and financial security if you don't have good health to enjoy those benefits. Most starkly, planning the me of tomorrow is meaningless if you don't get to tomorrow. As my friend RJ continually reminds me, "Without our health, we have nothing."

Of course, we are all subconsciously aware that this is in the lap of

THE ME OF TOMORROW

the gods, to some degree. Luck and genes are critical players in life's tableau. However, to a significant extent, most of us can take steps today to dramatically enhance our health of tomorrow and even our chances of reaching some of those many tomorrows. This chapter is about those steps—the levers we can pull to improve our destiny. While some of these steps are more obvious, such as eat well and exercise, I also want to add a couple that we often overlook: sleep well and manage stress.

WHAT CAN I CONTROL?

For most people with lucky genes and modern medicine, life expectancy at birth is roughly eighty years. Data published in 2019 by the United Nations Development Program shows a global range, from the midfifties in some African countries to over eighty-four in Japan and Hong Kong.[53] The 2017 CIA Factbook places the US forty-third in the world, at eighty years.[54]

Because you have already survived many perilous years and lived to enjoy many tomorrows, we can estimate that, by now, you have an excellent mathematical chance of going further—in fact, reaching your mideighties. Beyond that point, most people experience declining health. That decline can happen rapidly or slowly. Even after that, many people continue to defy time's sickle. As the Blue Zones studies in chapter 4 showed, physical and psychological factors play roles for those fortunate folks.

While our eventual fate may be beyond our control, science tells us that today's health choices can dramatically affect the pace of decline before our mideighties and the rate of decline beyond them. I call this the fifty-eighty curve. Evidence suggests that the decisions we make throughout our earlier years significantly change the curve's steepness from age fifty to eighty. The curve can either be

---
[53] http://hdr.undp.org/en/content/2019-human-development-index-ranking.
[54] https://www.cia.gov/library/publications/the-world-factbook/rankorder/2102rank.html.

relatively flat—with health declining only marginally until we reach those older years—or point severely downward, with increasing health problems and complications in late middle to old age. In order to enjoy those tomorrows we are planning for, we need to aim for the flattest-possible curve. The choices we make in our earlier years mold that shape dramatically.

The advice in this chapter is not a panacea for all that ails us. I do not prescribe pills or potions, endorse miracle cures, or recommend particular weight-loss regimens. Instead, my health advice is a broad approach to health and wellness based on data and experience. Much of this advice seems like common sense, but we all so often fail to do what's right and to stick to these tried and tested best practices. For this reason, this chapter offers a set of simple recommendations for a healthier life and a potential me of tomorrow, based on simple human observation and a dispassionate interpretation of the best available data and evidence.

Serious scientific research has consistently supported the view that some of the chronic diseases in the Western world can be avoided with a combination of lifestyle changes and a better diet. Therefore, we need to assert control and choice. We *can* affect what happens to us.[55]

Some readers might think that the tips in this chapter are obvious. If so, great—you are obviously health aware. However, most smart young professionals I know either are unaware of what's best for their health or routinely ignore it. After all, our health prospects between the ages of fifty and eighty aren't on our radar screens as we live our busy lives. However, these simple concepts are the cornerstones to maximizing your chance of getting to tomorrow and having a healthy life when you get there. It's no guarantee—nothing in life is—but ignoring these concepts will without question jeopardize your health for tomorrow.

---

[55] W. C. Willett, "Balancing Life-Style and Genomics Research for Disease Prevention," *Science* 296, no. 5568 (2002): 695–98, https://doi.org/10.1126/science.1071055.

WHAT ABOUT VIRUSES LIKE COVID-19?

A hundred days before I wrote this chapter, nobody on earth could have imagined how the subject of health would come to dominate our lives for so long after that. For months, public and private discourse was about little else than the global coronavirus pandemic. We discovered that the virus that caused the terrifying illness COVID-19 was almost perfectly malignant: highly contagious, spreading from asymptomatic and symptomatic people alike, affecting multiple bodily functions, and becoming fatal for some or debilitating for some of those who survived. And that's just a list of its health effects. The revolutionary rearrangements to our habits and lifestyles wreaked economic and social carnage around the world. We all knew deep down that life would never be the same.

There was horrifying randomness about the virus's attack. Making decisions even for the me of today became challenging and psychologically taxing, exacerbated by weak political direction and muddled public communication in many parts of the world. With governments appearing impotent, we increasingly felt we were out there on our own, making life-and-death decisions for ourselves and our families. Many of us devoured and dissected every scrap of information and research—every new theory or revelation from scientists and medical practitioners worldwide—to make smarter decisions for our health and that of our loved ones.

It quickly became apparent that this virus hit people with certain preexisting medical conditions hardest. Simply, people in poor health had a much higher probability of doing worse. By six months into the crisis, doctors in 216 countries had been battling the virus for more than one hundred days. Consequently, there was an emerging consensus about the most problematic conditions most associated with poor outcomes once exposed: chronic obstructive pulmonary disease, cardiovascular disease, diabetes, chronic kidney disease, and obesity.

A study used the CDC's Behavioral Risk Factor Surveillance System to measure the prevalence of these conditions in the US population.[56] This study shows that an extraordinary 40.7 percent of the US population has one or more of these conditions, making them especially vulnerable to poor health outcomes from the virus. The number one condition is obesity (30.9 percent), and the second is diabetes (11.1 percent). Sadly, both of these conditions are mostly preventable.

The coronavirus pandemic finally focused the world's attention, reminding us all that viruses and disease remain one of humanity's greatest threats. Just as in the case of COVID-19, the best weapons we currently have are our own immune systems. We know that the more robust our immune systems and the fewer preexisting medical conditions we have, the better our chances of surviving a random virus strike. Of course, some people have inherited conditions that make them vulnerable. However, the truth is that, sadly, most of the relevant preexisting medical conditions are largely avoidable. Sometimes genes and fate deal us a weak hand, but for most of us, managing our health will help us avoid the most dangerous preexisting conditions. Better health includes a more robust immune system to ward off disease. In my view, the root cause of these avoidable conditions is intrinsically linked to a lack of me-of-tomorrow thinking. This type of thinking will not just help us live better and more fulfilling lives. We now know that it is critical to our personal survival. Having a me-of-tomorrow-oriented health strategy has never been more vital.

---

[56] Hilda Razzaghi, Yan Wang, Hua Lu, et al., "Estimated County-Level Prevalence of Selected Underlying Medical Conditions Associated with Increased Risk for Severe COVID-19 Illness—United States, 2018," *Morbidity Mortality Weekly Report* 69, no. 29 (2020): 945–50, http://dx.doi.org/10.15585/mmwr.mm6929a1.

HEALTH COMPONENTS

There are four components to building our best-possible immune systems and being as healthy as possible:

1. Sleep
2. Stress management
3. Food
4. Exercise

These are the cornerstones for managing health for the me of tomorrow. I'd like to start with the two that we often overlook—sleep and stress management. In my judgment, they are just as important as the more commonly discussed elements—food and exercise.

Although we often muddy and complicate it, optimizing health is as simple as this. To reach a healthy tomorrow, you need to plan and manage these four areas of your life. This chapter will explore each of these in turn. It will offer some critical truths you need to internalize and some essential tips you need to master. Everything else is genes and fate.

SLEEP

> Sleep is the golden chain that ties health and our bodies together.
> —THOMAS DEKKER

Sleep is the least obvious of my four health guidelines and easily the most neglected. Many people who eat correctly and exercise regularly think they're doing enough to support their long-term health. Besides, too often, we view denying ourselves sleep as a badge of honor. We cast as heroes people who get up early, throw themselves into work, and then burn the midnight oil. I have worked with many people who say with pride, "I only need four or five hours of sleep." Popular culture often portrays the need for sleep as a sign of weakness, a waste of life's precious time. Tech companies like Facebook famously sponsor all-night "hackathons" fueled by copious quantities of Red Bull. As the quote attributed to American songwriter and musician Warren Zevon tells us, "I'll sleep when I'm dead."

There's no harm in pulling the occasional all-nighter or flinging your energy into a productive activity that temporarily deprives you of sleep. However, sleep science has uncovered some startling and little-known problems. We now know that sleep deprivation seriously jeopardizes health at both individual and societal levels. It creates colossal and often hidden public health problems. Simply, regularly getting inadequate sleep will have a catastrophic effect on your health of tomorrow. It is as damaging for your body and your immune system as eating poorly, neglecting exercise, and living a life of uncontrolled stress.

FOLLOW THE SCIENCE

Sleep science has advanced by leaps and bounds over the last few decades, although it got off to a relatively late start. It wasn't until the eighteenth century that the magic of circadian rhythms became known. This unique mechanism has been proven to exist in animals, plants, fungi, and even some types of bacteria. Only in the last century has scientific experimentation demonstrated that these rhythms are endogenous—that is, innate to organisms and independent of external stimuli. This rhythm is one of the two major factors that dictate your level of alertness and need for sleep; the other is the level of a chemical in your brain called adenosine.[57]

The phases of REM sleep—one of the cornerstones of mental

---

[57] Matthew Walker, *Why We Sleep: The New Science of Sleep and Dreams* (London: Penguin Books, 2018), 27.

and physical health—were only uncovered in 1953.[58] And it has only been in these last few decades that the training and accreditation programs necessary to develop a cadre of experts in the discipline of sleep medicine were established. Specialized sleep clinics and centers have mushroomed—there are now more than 4,700 in the US—and there are now physicians who can treat disorders like narcolepsy and hypersomnia.[59] However, the number of qualified physicians has not remotely kept pace with the seriousness of the widespread and destructive epidemic of sleep deprivation.

Given the scale of sleep deprivation's impact, progress has been painfully slow. It seems that the success and acclaim that accompanied Matthew Walker's *Why We Sleep* in 2017—one of my favorite books about sleep—show that it struck a nerve. People have started to appreciate the connection between sleep quality and overall health. Walker, professor of neuroscience and psychology at the University of California, Berkeley, researches the impact of sleep on human health and disease. My favorite passage in his book is when he extols the benefits of sleep: "Scientists have discovered a revolutionary new treatment that makes you live longer. It enhances your memory and makes you more creative. It makes you look more attractive. It keeps you slim and lowers food cravings. It protects you from cancer and dementia. It wards off colds and the flu. It lowers your risk of heart attacks and stroke, not to mention diabetes. You'll even feel happier, less depressed, and less anxious."

The consensus among experts like him—and he is not out on a limb with this analysis—is that adults between the ages of eighteen and sixty-five require seven hours of sleep per night. This recommendation has become the new standard for the CDC. Failure to meet this level has extensive destructive effects not just for brain function and risk of dementia but also for the cardiovascular system,

---

[58] Nathaniel F. Watson and others, "The Past Is Prologue: The Future of Sleep Medicine," *Journal of Clinical Sleep Medicine* 13, no. 1 (2017): 127–35, https://doi.org/10.5664/jcsm.6406.

[59] https://blog.marketresearch.com/top-6-things-to-know-about-the-28-billion-sleep-market.

the metabolism, the reproductive system, and—crucial in the time of viruses—the immune system. Walker expertly details the evidence in his work, and other researchers have also identified this as a global problem.[60]

In my experience, most people in their twenties and thirties think that four to five hours of sleep per night is OK. When they talk about sleep, they routinely measure the total time in bed, not the amount of time actually spent sleeping. Statistics from the CDC bear this out. Their 2014 Behavioral Risk Factor Surveillance System shows that more than 35 percent of all adults fail to achieve a minimum of seven hours regularly.[61] Among those aged twenty-five to forty-four—when me-of-tomorrow thinking can have such a major impact—the proportion is more than 38 percent.

The human and social costs of this are vast. A study by the RAND Corporation estimates that the US financial impact alone is more than $411 billion annually.[62] The effect on individual health and well-being has also been well documented. Neglecting sleep is one of the surest ways to imperil your healthy tomorrow.

Aside from these me-of-tomorrow benefits, sleep directly impacts our lives and performance today. In a 2018 *Harvard Business Review* article, Christopher Barnes synthesized a series of studies demonstrating the benefits of adequate sleep for various aspects of business and workplace performance.[63] Sleep deprivation causes both leadership quality and manager-employer relationships to suffer—managers' ability to inspire and motivate declines. Furthermore, leaders who communicate what the researchers' term "sleep devaluation"—encouraging their teams to work long hours and

---

[60] Vijay Kumar Chattu and others, "The Global Problem of Insufficient Sleep and Its Serious Public Health Implications," *Healthcare* 7, no. 1 (2018): 1, https://doi.org/10.3390/healthcare7010001; Walker, *Why We Sleep*, 164–89.

[61] https://www.cdc.gov/sleep/data_statistics.html.

[62] Marco Hafner, Martin Stepanek, Jirka Taylor, Wendy M. Troxel, and Christian Van Stolk, "Why Sleep Matters—the Economic Costs of Insufficient Sleep: A Cross-Country Comparative Analysis" (Santa Monica: RAND Corporation, 2016), https://www.rand.org/pubs/research_reports/RR1791.html.

[63] https://hbr.org/2018/09/sleep-well-lead-better.

sacrifice sleep—directly impact their subordinates' quality of rest and, interestingly, and their ability to behave ethically. Sleep deprivation generally has been shown to create lapses in ethics in organizations.

MY SLEEP GUIDELINES

For both the me of today and the me of tomorrow, I consider getting adequate sleep a priority equal to eating well and exercising regularly. However, before researching the subject, I was blissfully unaware of its health significance. After investigating further and dissecting plenty of sleep data, I created a personal plan. This plan applies to regular days at home or when I can control my sleeping environment. Sometimes this is difficult when traveling; obviously, some days are exceptions. During the COVID-19 pandemic, it became more the rule than the exception. For simplicity's sake, the plan evolved into the following six simple rules:

1. **Create an eight-hour sleep opportunity.** This means scheduling eight uninterrupted hours in bed. If you allow extra time to decompress, fall asleep, and occasionally wake with sleeping rhythms or nocturnal bathroom trips, this provides a high degree of probability of achieving the minimum required seven hours of sleep every day.
2. **Head to bed at approximately the same time every day.** Some people swear by this and stick to it even when depriving themselves of their eight-hour opportunity. I try to combine it with rule 1. It also requires getting up at the same time every day. Data shows that this kind of regularity anchors the circadian rhythm, which is always marginally misaligned from a twenty-four-hour clock. Several small studies suggest that this regularity cuts down on time spent

in bed tossing and turning before drifting off.[64] It's worked for me!

3. **Don't eat too late.** There's nothing like a bout of indigestion to dash those best-laid plans for a refreshing night's sleep. I aim to finish dinner, including drinks, at least two to three hours before bed. The beneficial nightcap is a myth—it will hinder, not help, a good night's sleep—although caffeine-free beverages and water are OK in these final hours.

4. **Avoid late-night screen time.** According to the Sleep Foundation, 90 percent of people in the US use electronic screens during the hour before bedtime.[65] The organization's research shows that the short-wavelength artificial blue light suppresses melatonin—a crucial chemical that makes us sleepy. As a reading junkie, I found this particularly difficult, as so much of my reading library was on my tablet. I shifted to listening to Audible and reading old-fashioned paper books. The switch took time, but now my devices are tucked away ninety minutes before bed.

5. **Learn to put yourself back to sleep.** Nearly all of us wake up periodically during the night as we cycle through sleep's different phases. Some of us either are only peripherally aware of waking or can easily fall back to sleep. However, like many people, I never found getting back to sleep easy. As you've probably gathered, my brain doesn't switch off easily. Once it's kick-started, even if I've only engaged first gear, ideas start buzzing around and my planning gene takes over. I can't claim these nocturnal schemes were ever worth much when confronted by the cold light of day. Still, the process of creating them meant that seven hours was often unattainable. Consequently, I focused on practicing techniques to get

---

[64] C. L. Finley and B. J. Cowley, "The Effects of a Consistent Sleep Schedule on Time Taken to Achieve Sleep," *Clinical Case Studies* 4, no. 3 (2005): 304–11, https://doi.org/10.1177/1534650103259743.

[65] https://www.sleepfoundation.org/articles/why-electronics-may-stimulate-you-bed.

myself back to sleep. One tried and trusted method is meditation, which I discuss in the next section; however, I learned other simple tricks, such as learning how to empty my mind. One of the most intriguing is a drumming-and-breathing exercise championed by musician and educator Jim Donovan.[66] A word of caution: ultimately, none of the techniques work unless you pay simultaneous attention to the three other components of health—food, exercise, and stress management. All these components complement one another.

6. **Watch how you sleep.** Most of us think that we have a decent handle on how we sleep—that we can wake up in the morning and pretty much tell whether we got anywhere close to seven hours. Actually, research suggests that people aren't good at estimating the time it takes them to get to sleep or the amount of sleep they get. One typical example was highlighted in a paper by two sleep researchers in the UK, showing how insomniacs misperceive both the time it takes them to get to sleep and the time they do sleep.[67] My point is not to question the extent of sleep deprivation relative to need—there's no disputing that evidence—but to indicate that without technological assistance, people are bad at estimating how much proper shut-eye they get. I have become religious about measuring my sleep because, as I shared in the previous chapter, I learned from Peter Drucker that if you can't measure it, you can't improve it. It's my way of ensuring that I achieve my seven-hour-per-night goal. I use a handy device called the Oura Ring. Modern Fitbit models play a similar role, and Apple Watch apps have similar functionality. If getting your seven hours and staying asleep is not your problem, these devices may sound like overkill;

---

[66] https://www.youtube.com/watch?v=A5dE25ANU0k.
[67] Allison G. Harvey and Nicole K. Y. Tang, "(Mis)perception of Sleep in Insomnia: A Puzzle and a Resolution," Psychological Bulletin 138, no. 1 (2012): 77–101.

however, I find the data illuminating and hugely helpful in establishing patterns and making sleep the priority it must be. I find that I can develop correlations and see how my sleep is impacted when I drink alcohol or eat late in the day.

These six rules work for me, but experts like Matthew Walker detail many other tips and tricks to conquer sleep's challenges, such as an unwinding period and a hot bath. I settled on these six as the easiest to execute, the most practical, and the most effective for sleep quality—and hence my overall health for tomorrow.

STRESS MANAGEMENT

My second health imperative is another one we often neglect, but it is an equally critical component for the health of tomorrow. While intrinsically liked to the other three health imperatives, it's so important to me that it deserves separate attention.

In recent years, stress has become another major focus for individual and public health improvement. What makes stress especially tricky is that it's a double-edged sword. Some level of stress is necessary for motivation and achievement. Not only is it an unavoidable element of life, but it also has physiological and psychological benefits that improve vital bodily functions and produce optimal performance, mentally and physically.

Many people suggest removing stress is an understandable reaction to the high-pressure nature of modern life, but this idea is neither possible nor beneficial. The secret isn't the elimination of stress: it's understanding how to manage it. Stress will always be with us; we just have to understand it, confront it, and know that it's another life challenge to manage alongside many others.

THE EFFECTS OF STRESS

Don't think I'm giving stress a bit of a free pass. On the contrary, it's a colossal mistake to deny its powerful impact on our short- and long-term health. Recent research on its physiological toxicity showcases its power. Sadly, many of us have witnessed friends or family members suffer from a most visible and often tragic manifestation—a sudden premature heart attack.

During periods of stress, the brain's hypothalamus releases hormones that create the classic fight-or-flight response, wired into humans since our ancestors lived in caves. A short list of the physiological impact is actually quite long: headaches, depression, heartburn, insomnia, shortness of breath, elevated blood sugar, escalated heart rate, blood pressure that increases heart attack risk, muscle tension leading to backaches, fertility problems, missed periods, stomachaches and digestive disorders, low sex drive, and erectile dysfunction. If that's not enough, stress weakens the immune system, leaving our bodies vulnerable to infection and killer viruses.

No serious medical practitioner would question the role of stress in any of these conditions. It has now become common knowledge. Many years ago, a friend told me the story of how his father, during a work-related crisis, visited his old family doctor complaining of several of these ailments. The doctor's advice was odd but useful: get a dog! The obvious diagnosis was stress. The doctor felt that a combination of exercising the dog and refocusing the patient's attention to his new pet would help change his mindset and manage his condition.

So we know that stress is a killer. Unmanaged, it wreaks havoc on many of the body's vital systems. Even if you survive its worst effects today, stress sets your body up for long-term damage and an unhealthy tomorrow. Managing stress, not eliminating it, is the key.

The first step in managing stress is understanding stress—what it does to your body and how it's impacting you. The cause of those headaches or digestive pains, or even your eating disorder or hair loss, is not always apparent. Perhaps it's a rare or complicated illness requiring diagnosis and treatment, but more likely, it's a physical manifestation of your brain continually preparing your fight-or-flight response.

MANAGING STRESS

Since stress is unavoidable, we must all learn to manage it. Most of us recognize stress, although it can often be so pervasive it hardly registers. When we think of stressful events, our minds turn to big events: losing a job, breaking up with a partner, experiencing the death of a loved one, undergoing surgery, and the like. Yet recent research has found that even seemingly small stressors can damage our long-term health. Sometimes, holding on to an unresolved issue is enough to trigger those physiological reactions that lead to long-term damage. One study by a group of academics at the University of California, Irvine, showed how a negative effect lingering the day after even a minor stressor is associated with future health problems and disease susceptibility.[68] The researchers explain how the impact of even minor stressors such as arguments linger through the following day—creating rumination and worry—and how that recovery phase itself contributes to future health conditions. Their conclusion showcases the importance of that age-old advice "Let it go!" but it also demonstrates how difficult it is to follow that counsel.

Sometimes we create unnecessary stress for ourselves by generating background noise for our psyche. I've thought about this on my various road trips across America. Like many fellow motorists, I used to drive at 10 percent over the speed limit when road conditions were good, a speed fast enough to generate a nagging background fear of getting a ticket. After a while, I noticed that this concern was ever present. This worry wasn't stress itself but was

---

[68] Kate A. Leger, Susan T. Charles, and David M. Almeida, "Let It Go: Lingering Negative Affect in Response to Daily Stressors Is Associated with Physical Health Years Later," *Psychological Science* 29, no. 8 (2018): 1283–90, https://doi.org/10.1177/0956797618763097.

similar to the background rumination and worry those California academics observed in people the day after an argument, with its observable negative health effect. It was like a background hum on the brain as the miles rolled past, reminding me of that small but ever-present risk. Simply by resetting cruise control to a speed closer to the limit, I found that slight anxiety evaporated. Long-distance driving can be challenging enough without the need to drain our stress batteries unnecessarily.

LETTING GO OF "TRUTHS"

We play psychological tricks on ourselves every day of our lives. Some of these tricks work for us; others become vital sources of stress. We all have our individual triggers—that is, what stresses one person might be water off a duck's back to another. And isn't it curious how we can all diagnose our friends' problems better than our own?

Letting go doesn't just apply to short-term stressors. Often, there are deep-seated psychological issues that have an insidious, stressful effect on our bodies. One unnecessary stressor relates to our own unique versions of the truth. Every day, we tell ourselves "truths" that we *think* we need to live by. Using a simple example, I may believe I *must* have a $100,000, $150,000, or $200,000 salary. This becomes my intrinsic truth. If I don't achieve that, I have failed myself, my family, my boss, the universe itself.

As a consequence, if I fail, my body generates continual low-level stress. The stress comes from the perceived failure to achieve that truth—something so ingrained in my psyche that it's not open to rational debate. We all have some of such truths central to our well-being—not necessarily financial, as in this example, but equally powerful and ingrained. These truths—different for everyone—are massive sources of stress.

One technique I recommend for letting go of these truths is to undertake a simple writing exercise. Complete the following three statements, listing up to three items for each:

- I can only be happy if ...
- I am afraid of ...
- I don't like it when ...

Sit down and review your statements. Think about them rationally. Put on a different set of glasses, and look at each one dispassionately. How logical are they? How accurate are these statements?

What you quickly realize is that the truths that seemed so self-evident were generated in your mind. They are stifling you. Instead of motivators, they have become inhibitors. It's time to let them go. If you're able to look at each truth and put it into perspective, it will help you let it go. Letting go provides freedom. This isn't laziness—it's liberation!

PERSONALIZING YOUR TECHNIQUES

In recent years, many age-old stress-management tools have become more mainstream. The antecedents of stress-management techniques are timeless. We know that meditation has been around for at least five thousand years. It was expressed in Hindu texts from around 1500 BC, evolving later in Taoist and Buddhist traditions.

Whether these practices were overt attempts to manage the stress of life is unclear, but the tools and techniques underpin many modern equivalents, such as Transcendental Meditation, famously popularized by Maharishi Mahesh Yogi in the 1960s. There are even connections to and overlaps with the contemporary practice of mindfulness, although purists will tell you they are not the same.

Dr. Herbert Benson elucidated the scientific benefits of meditation as a technique to manage stress in *The Relaxation Response*, first published in 1975.[69] Benson made several startling claims about the effects of stress on the human body, claiming that more than 60 percent of all health care providers' visits are related to stress.

---

[69] Herbert Benson and Miriam Z. Klipper, *The Relaxation Response*, updated and expanded ed. (New York: Quill, 2001).

His experiments demonstrated dramatic and rapid reductions in blood pressure and metabolic rate after periods of meditation. This little book has since sold more than six million copies and is still recommended by clinical psychologists today. Benson advocates a simple form of meditation as a proven way of eliciting the relaxation response and combating the effects of stress.

Yoga—seemingly one of today's most prominent antistress trends—has a similarly ancient history. According to the International Yoga Federation, there are now more than three hundred million practitioners across the globe. Somewhere around thirty-six million of them are Americans, up from fewer than eighteen million in 2008—a staggering increase in a single decade. This trend shows no sign of diminishing, as people appreciate the multiple health and overall fitness benefits that the practice reinforces.

Neither yoga nor meditation was a natural fit for my personality when I first got curious about how to manage my stress. However, the increasing number of adherents to meditation, yoga, mindfulness, and similar techniques is a sure testament to their power and effectiveness. Athletes like LeBron James, Stephen Curry, Lionel Messi, and Cristiano Ronaldo are known meditators. Personalities such as Bill Gates, Jerry Seinfeld, and Marc Benioff practice it. It has now become so easy to practice meditation with apps like Calm and Headspace, and there are meditation playlists in every favorite audio streaming service. Ways to reduce our stress are at our fingertips more than ever before. If you want to learn more, there are series on Netflix on the merits of slowing down and looking inside.

I believe developing your own personal stress-management tool kit is essential for reaching tomorrow and enjoying good physical and mental health later in life. My message is that everybody needs to develop a stress-management plan that works for him or her. This plan is as essential as food, exercise, and sleep, but it must be individualized and personal. The mental side of your health is as important as the physical. Both require forethought and planning.

FOOD

> Dis-moi ce que tu manges, je te dirai ce que tu es. (Tell me what you eat, and I'll tell you who you are.)
>
> —ANTHELME BRILLAT-SAVARIN

We all know people who seem to have been on diets their whole adult lives. I have friends who stack their bookshelves with every new nutrition book and know the details of every new fad diet. The most intriguing clickbait headlines are usually something like "Top Ten Eating Tips," or they promise the first reveal of a study touting the benefits of this or that allegedly new eating plan.

When it comes to food, we are all suckers for a new idea. We look for tricks and shortcuts to trim off the excess pounds, detonate our energy, pump up our muscles, or protect us from every ailment. These habits predate our new virus obsession I referred to earlier.

This information bombardment contributes to an atmosphere of profound confusion. We feel like there's too much data, too many choices, and too many competing opinions. From the 1971 breakthrough book *Diet for a Small Planet* through Michael Pollan's 2006 classic *The Omnivore's Dilemma* and hundreds of offerings since, doctors, nutritionists, and sometimes outright quacks have generated thousands of permutations of dietary regimens.[70]

However, despite the ubiquity of this wisdom and modern medicine's advanced physiological blueprints, most people consistently fail to appreciate Brillat-Savarin's simple truism: you are what you eat! What you ingest through your mouth is, to a very great degree, your health destiny. The key to your immune system's miraculous and complex functioning and your possibilities of healthy longevity lies not in pills and potions or special supplemental vitamins and minerals you ingest but in what you *choose* to eat as your essential diet.

By the way, the choice of what you ingest applies equally to

---

[70] Frances Moore Lappé and Marika Hahn, *Diet for a Small Planet* (New York: Ballantine Books, 2010); Michael Pollan, *The Omnivore's Dilemma: A Natural History of Four Meals* (New York: Penguin Press, 2006).

substances other than food. Any drinks, pills, and potions we consume define what we are and, crucially, what we will become. We need to take control of everything that enters our bodies: food, drink, and medicine. Many people laugh at the saying "Treat your body like a temple." But although we shouldn't worship them, in a genuine sense, our bodies—the only ones we will ever have—are so vital to our future well-being that we owe it to ourselves to be deliberate about anything passing our lips. If our cars can no longer run, we can get other ones. If our houses burn down, we can go and live somewhere else. We can get new computers, phones, shoes, or cameras, but if something happens to the vessels we have to navigate life, we just can't order new ones on Amazon!

Most of us know this applies to smoking and drugs, prescribed and nonprescribed kinds. There's enough available information about the risks of mind-altering substances. It's just never smart to jeopardize our future mental and physical health for questionable short-term gratification. Ingesting a substance without considering the effects is a simple contradiction of me-of-tomorrow thinking. Thankfully, in the case of alcohol, our bodies have developed a smart way of punishing us the following morning. In a literal sense, the me of tomorrow will pay the price!

A MATTER OF CHOICE

I mentioned that what food you eat is a choice. However, more accurately, our problems often arise from a *failure to choose*. One of the most fundamental problems with nutrition is not a lack of information but a lack of thought. It's the same failure of foresight that disregards the future me. The baleful impact of a junk food habit or a penchant for ice cream may not manifest itself for twenty or thirty years. But be sure: when it comes to the effects of diet on your heath, the chickens will come home to roost (in some cases, literally!).

What you put into your body will directly affect your health and well-being. Perhaps not today, or the literal tomorrow, but at another tomorrow to come. Therefore, my first rule of eating is to be mindful at all times of everything you put through your buccal cavity and into your temple of a body. The fuel you ingest will shape the contours of your biological future. This rule applies to every single bite. It doesn't mean you can't *choose* a bowl of ice cream or a slab of chocolate. It means you must consume it consciously, knowingly, willingly.

Regrettably, rather than developing the habit of making conscious dietary decisions, we often outsource it. And we sometimes outsource these elemental decisions to people who don't know our bodies and certainly don't live in them: maybe a food company, a fast-food restaurant, or even a well-meaning friend or family member. We relinquish this most vital of choices because of convenience, weariness, or stress. Just because fried chicken or pizza is the easiest, fastest, or tastiest meal to obtain, or the most available when we're hungry, it doesn't make it the right food choice for either the me of today or the me of tomorrow. Food selection is too significant to leave to others. You decide what to eat—and let science and research guide your thinking.

EXAMINING THE EVIDENCE

Our food choices should be guided first and foremost by evidence. Like every one of life's rational decisions (although, as we know, not all are), we need to trust the data and science. When it's overwhelming, connect the dots. Don't trust an individual with spurious claims about his or her unique diet solution or a random study of a dozen unique patients. Move from the general to the specific, not the other way around. Trust the *weight* of evidence.

Another critical note on evidence: examine the source critically. An examination doesn't necessarily mean questioning the author's credentials—although many MDs claim nutritional expertise when their specialism lies elsewhere. It is more about who commissions and funds a particular study. It's not unduly cynical to appreciate that people promote ideas that benefit them or their stakeholders' interests—that's standard business practice and universal human nature.

One prominent example of questionable authorship comes from a half century ago. A body called the Sugar Research Foundation responded to a series of studies that emerged in the 1950s linking sugar consumption with coronary arterial disease.[71] Over the following decade, that organization, funded by sugar producers, commissioned a series of alternative studies that squarely shifted public attention to fat and dietary cholesterol as the main culprits. Documentary evidence shows that this was a coordinated campaign.

By the 1980s, most scientists had signed on to this new orthodoxy. The 1980 Dietary Guidelines for Americans focused on reducing total fat, saturated fat, and dietary cholesterol to prevent coronary arterial disease, ignoring all the earlier research naming sugar as a primary culprit.

One consequence of this coordinated campaign was that the consumption of sugar and high-fructose corn syrup skyrocketed. Mission accomplished, so to speak. Similarly, the battle between low-carb and low-fat diets that has raged over the last twenty years has been influenced to a considerable degree by various agricultural interest groups.[72]

Unfortunately, obesity, diabetes, and heart disease rates went in the same direction as sugar consumption and have never been higher. Research published in 2014 showed that over the last three decades, the amount of "added sugar" Americans consumed had risen by more than 30 percent.[73] These sugars and syrups (often corn syrup)

---

[71] Cristin E. Kearns, Laura A. Schmidt, and Stanton A. Glantz, "Sugar Industry and Coronary Heart Disease Research: A Historical Analysis of Internal Industry Documents," *JAMA Internal Medicine* 176, no. 11 (2016): 1680–85, https://doi.org/10.1001/jamainternmed.2016.5394.

[72] https://www.pcrm.org/news/blog/dangers-industry-influenced-nutrition-research.

[73] https://www.sciencedaily.com/releases/2014/11/141104141731.htm.

are added into foods and drinks during preparation or processing, over and above the sugars that naturally occur in fruit or dairy foods.

As Michael Moss described in his award-winning book *Salt, Sugar, Fat: How the Food Giants Hooked Us*, food companies are consciously culpable in this increase in disease.[74] They carefully manufacture a balance of these three elements to maximize psychological pleasure and hook consumers in the full knowledge of the harmful effects. Thankfully, labeling requirements and greater public awareness now give us a choice. It is one that we need to learn to exercise. The lesson here is that outsourcing our food choices to food manufacturers can lead us sadly astray.

I think it is essential to understand an inconvenient truth that applies equally to food and work life, as I discussed in chapter 2 (Me @ Work). Just as any employer won't prioritize your well-being, neither will large food conglomerates. Their shareholders come first, and they will do everything in their power to further two objectives: (1) get you to consumer more and (2) lower their costs.

Making food saltier or sweeter will help accomplish that first objective. To further that goal, they employ teams of food scientists dedicated to using chemistry to create new and improved flavors. They also add ingredients to make foods more visually appealing.

To accomplish the second objective, lower production and inventory expenses—food companies also add ingredients to make foods stay fresher for longer. They are looking out for their shareholders, so it's up to us to look out for our health, which means understanding how those extra ingredients that make sense for the manufacturers impact us.

THE CHINA STUDY

Easily the most comprehensive scientific nutritional research ever undertaken is what has become known as the China Study. This

---

[74] Michael Moss, *Salt, Sugar, Fat: How the Food Giants Hooked Us* (Toronto: Signal, 2013).

twenty-year study, otherwise known as the China-Cornell-Oxford project, was conducted by the Chinese Academy of Preventive Medicine, Cornell University, and the University of Oxford. The *New York Times* described it as "the Grand Prix of epidemiology." Published as a book in 2005 by father-and-son duo Colin and Tom Campbell, it's an extensive analysis of nutritional and disease patterns in rural China. Even today, it remains one of the most important studies about diet and health ever completed.[75]

The China Study provided an overwhelming weight of evidence demonstrating how animal-protein intake correlates with modern disease patterns. The primary finding was that in areas of rural China with limited animal-protein availability, rates of many modern diseases such as heart disease and cancer were one-tenth of those in places where people consumed animal protein.

Dr. Campbell and his colleagues then moved from the general to the specific. They tested plant-based diets with their own cardiac patients at Cornell. This part of the research demonstrated how to reverse heart disease and diabetes by eliminating animal protein and dairy products altogether.

This study was not a one-off quick fix to the problem of escalating heart disease, diabetes, and cancer in Western societies. It was a comprehensive analysis of reams of data backed up by years of medical treatment in a world-class facility. Although other nutritionists challenged these conclusions, nobody seriously questioned the data or evidence on which these conclusions are based. The study was observational: consequently, it shows relationships between the variables measured rather than proving cause and effect. However, the sheer weight of evidence convinced me. Even if causation is unproven, correlations are undeniable.

The most common attack on the implications of the China Study came from proponents of what is sometimes called the Paleolithic or

---

[75] T. Colin Campbell and Thomas M. Campbell, *The China Study: The Most Comprehensive Study of Nutrition Ever Conducted and the Startling Implications for Diet, Weight Loss and Long-Term Health*, 1st BenBella Books ed. (Dallas: BenBella Books, 2005).

Paleo diet. Advocates of this eating style believe human beings should eat more like our hunter-gatherer ancestors, insofar as scientists can understand their dietary preferences from the fossil record. Hence this plan includes meat and fish as core elements of the diet. The advocates' theory, known as the discordance hypothesis, contends that the current human diet is genetically mismatched from our evolutionary eating patterns. Intellectually satisfying though this theory is, it lacks the weight of evidence associated with the proven health benefits of plant-based eating. The most significant public health challenge in Western societies is what we call *modern-day* diseases, such as cancer, heart disease, and diabetes. Evidence indicates that plant-based eating plans address these challenges better.

Interestingly, these otherwise contrasting approaches have some crucial things in common. Both advocate natural rather than processed food. Both are united on three critical issues:

1. The importance of vegetables
2. The need to eliminate pure sugar from our diet
3. The benefits of avoiding or removing dairy products from our diet

Perhaps we can leave the last word on diet approaches to Michael Pollan. In the succinct summary of his book *In Defense of Food*, the sequel to *The Omnivore's Dilemma*, he summarizes it beautifully: "Eat food. Not too much. Mostly plants."[76]

MY NUTRITIONAL PRINCIPLES

I believe everyone should choose a nutritional plan that works best for his or her own heath of tomorrow. The emphasis has to be on the word *choice*.

First, decide on your health objectives. At a minimum, they

---

[76] Michael Pollan, *In Defense of Food: An Eater's Manifesto* (New York: Penguin Press, 2008), 1.

should be to optimize your immune system for the me of today and build better cardiovascular health and cancer-fighting properties for the me of tomorrow. These are the developed world's two major killers. I know where I stand on this evidence.

Second, make sure your plan has a good chance of success. Take account of your lifestyle, location, food availability, and budget. There's little point in creating an eating plan that becomes too onerous for your time or wallet. Thankfully, that's not too much of a problem for most of us, but it's critical.

My path to better health and nutrition was something of a roundabout journey. Although I had always been mindful of the need to eat well and exercise, my true journey started when my annual physical revealed that I was already accumulating plaque in my arteries. It wasn't much, but the doctor alerted me that the process had started. I knew heart disease ran in my family; the main driver for starting down this path was tomorrow orientation. I knew that to prevent my health from falling off a cliff after age fifty, I would need to build a robust immune system and a disease-fighting body.

Realizing in my early forties that life was finite drove me to research more about how food affects the body and how I could take better care of it—my me-of-tomorrow thinking kicked in. One key driver was my desire to avoid taking medicines to lower my cholesterol, as the doctor had suggested. I had read about the side effects of statins, so I decided I wouldn't use big pharma's solution to my problem unless I absolutely had to do it. I read books, watched documentaries, and listened to podcasts. Based on these objectives, my new journey embraced four basic principles.

1. **Eliminate dairy products—milk, cheese, butter, and yogurt.**

    > This was hard for me and continues to be, but I know it is right to do it. This idea aligns with the principles of plant-based-eating advocates and paleo dieticians alike. Evidence suggests that the human body is not conditioned to consume a substance created

for calves. Despite the long-standing use of all these products in Western societies over the last several centuries, another clue lies in the high incidences of lactose intolerance and other allergies evident in milk-consuming societies.

The prevalence of milk-based products is another case of a highly successful pressure group—in this case, the dairy industry—successfully manipulating public perception, even to the extent of mandating milk consumption for children. Dairy is ubiquitous; consequently, its sheer prevalence makes elimination a principle rather than a mandate. When I first stopped using dairy, I quickly noticed some of my nagging allergies went away. Although I can't prove causation, at a minimum there is a correlation.

The good news is that now there are so many choices for those occasions where you think only dairy will do: almond and oat products work well, as well as coconut milk—my least favorite because of its fat content.

2. **Reduce meat and fish consumption.**

This principle is the most significant takeaway from the China Study and the one that caused my most significant dietary transformation. As a former steak connoisseur, I gradually weaned myself off beef first, followed by pork. Living in Texas at the time, I was an enthusiastic griller of baby back ribs and something of a barbecue aficionado. This practice had to stop, which created a social change that even my close friends didn't understand or appreciate. Now, if I have animal protein at all, I choose either chicken or fish, but I try to eat vegetarian whenever possible. I have made it a point to find and catalog restaurants that cater to vegetarians and support them as often as possible. Although my goal is the health of tomorrow, this has also dramatically improved my health of today. I found that the health benefits manifest themselves remarkably quickly.

3. **Limit sugar.**

   I was also a fan of desserts—especially my traditional dishes like dulce de leche. My mouth's need for sugar seemed like a physical necessity. The trick in taming this compulsion was not to fight that immediate sugar urge. Instead, I ordered my favorite dessert but trained myself to have only one or, at most, two bites and then send it back. Wasteful, you might say, but it controlled my sugar fix. My cravings dissipated surprisingly rapidly.

   Like dairy, sugar remains ubiquitous in the Western diet. It's almost impossible to eliminate completely. I don't challenge restaurant waiters or avoid everything with a hint of sugar, but items like sugary drinks were easy to dispense with. Now I reserve my dessert consumption for special occasions. The sugar glutton of yesterday quickly morphed into the occasional indulger. Ice cream is now to me the same special treat it was to me when I was a child.

4. **Do the best you can to avoid processed foods.**

   My rationale is pretty straightforward. When food is sold in a box, can, or bag, the manufacturer needs to ensure it will stay fresh for a long time. The reason is simple: it needs to go from a factory to a distribution center to a store to your home and then sit on a shelf waiting for you to consume it. For that purpose, the manufacturer has to add ingredients that are not part of the food but intended to ensure the food looks good, tastes good, and does not harm you days or even weeks after purchase. My thinking is that if I can avoid ingredients that are for purposes other than to provide my body with nutrients, why not avoid them? As stated before, I only have one vessel, so I have an incentive to keep it in great shape. Just as I put the right type of gas and oil in my car, why not take care of myself in the same way?

ADJUSTING YOUR DIET

These stories might suggest I changed decades of eating habits at the flip of a switch. In fact, the opposite is true. As millions of dieters can attest, long-term dietary changes are always tricky. Often, the combination of food availability and lack of willpower torpedo our best-laid plans. Daily stress and time pressure compel us to revert to tried and tested menus, even though we know they are unhealthy.

My experience in establishing new eating habits taught me that although some people swear by it, cold turkey doesn't work well. The best method is to make changes by degrees. Cold turkey works for a while, but when we face impossible choices, it's an excuse to revert, and it's hard to resurrect that purity of purpose. As James Clear brilliantly summarizes in his *Atomic Habits*, tiny changes yield remarkable results.[77] The process is as important as the goal. You should gradually and methodically add or eliminate items from your shopping lists and restaurant choices until you fine-tune your system for success. This was my personal method of modifying my diet.

When I decided on the first principle—eliminating dairy products—I hit a severe roadblock. I thought I was in love with cheese. It's easy to do, especially given the depth and variety of options available today, compared to the shrink-wrapped rubbery cheese many of us grew up with. So I analyzed my habits and patterns. When and under what circumstances did I consume most of my cheese? What were the occasions, and what were the accompanying food items? I realized that my most pleasurable cheese-eating episodes were not in the everyday home or restaurant meals but in the hors d'oeuvres we'd serve at home when we had guests over for lunch or dinner. Wine was usually involved. Therefore, I realized that most of my enjoyment of cheese was not so much about its texture and taste but about the spirit of the occasion, the conversation with guests, and the pleasure of relaxing over a glass of wine after a hard week. Most

---

[77] James Clear, *Atomic Habits: Tiny Changes, Remarkable Results—an Easy and Proven Way to Build Good Habits and Break Bad Ones* (New York: Avery, 2018).

of the joy was in the event, not the food itself. If I could re-create the occasion with an alternative hors d'oeuvre, it would barely diminish my pleasure.

I looked for healthier food that could fulfill the same social function and landed on one that is popular, easy to make, versatile and that comes in all kinds of flavors: many of the same qualities of cheese. I switched allegiance to hummus and fell in love with that instead. It's also fun to make, tweaking ingredients and different spices in front of a blender. Another side benefit is that you can enjoy hummus just as easily accompanied by vegetables rather than crackers. For me, it became a pleasurable vehicle for those vital plant foods my new eating plan required.

Like my abandonment of red meat, I confess that this adjustment took some time, and my cheese divorce required a few interim steps. When I felt my former ruler's tug, I sometimes compromised with alternatives like Laughing Cow low-fat cheese spread and low-fat string cheese. Although initially, life after cheese wasn't easy, it didn't take long to transition fully.

This breakup was a crucial way station on my dairy-free, mostly plant-centric journey. It allowed me to avoid tempting stalwarts like pizza, parmesan on pasta, cheese ravioli, and cheese with omelets. Through this kind of systematic, planned approach, you can evolve toward a better diet for tomorrow with incalculable benefits for your long-term health.

WEIGHING YOURSELF EVERY DAY

Most of us can recite several numbers with a degree of accuracy. Perhaps our college GPAs or degree classifications, our social security numbers, and maybe even our bank account numbers (and perhaps balances). This information is a constant mental companion. In former times, it included phone numbers of our spouses, partners, and parents—of course, those days are long gone! However, another number that we should recall without thinking is more important than any of these: our weight.

Obviously, health is about much more than weight. However, weight is a good proxy for fitness and an excellent one for dietary progress. My trusty bathroom scale is the one simple tool that manages my sense of urgency about food and exercise. I know many will argue, correctly, that many people have a "correct" weight and body mass index (BMI) but are unhealthy or are far from the "correct" weight or BMI but in good health. Most of these people know who they are.

The daily weighing habit applies to the vast majority of us who have felt the nagging concern of a weight problem at some time in our lives. As a result, we changed our eating habits and increased our exercise. One way for us to stay true to our new practices is to have our weight fresh in our minds every day. Keeping it top of mind helps us get more motivated to eat the right food, consume the right amount of food, and exercise regularly.

Weighing myself daily helped me understand which foods impact me more. As a simple example, I started using oatmeal as a breakfast cereal to manage my cholesterol level. As much as I enjoyed it, mixed with berries and honey every day, I found my weight creeping up. Switching to Cheerios actually made my weight come back down. It was only a small variance of three or four pounds, but once I uncovered this secret, I made that adjustment. Without that daily monitoring tool, the realization might have come ten pounds later, when I realized my pants were too tight.

Here are a few considerations about a daily weighing regime:

- Try to weigh yourself at the same time every day. Right after waking up or after a shower works best. If it's before breakfast one day, don't make it after breakfast the next. You need to keep everything consistent.
- Don't let small fluctuations discourage you. The dinner you had or the liquid you drank the night before can have a small but significant impact.

- Record your number. Either write it down in a notebook or use an app like MyFitnessPal. This record allows you to keep track months later and monitor progress over long periods. There's nothing more rewarding than seeing massive progress that was built on tiny increments.
- Remember that muscle weighs more than fat. As you increase your exercise, you will build muscle mass, and your weight will naturally increase. However, if you're like most of us, the increase attributable to muscle mass will be small, so don't kid yourself those extra few pounds are because your overindulged on exercise rather than food!

Maintaining a healthy weight is just as challenging as losing it in the first place. That daily weighing habit will help keep your progress top of mind. Knowing that number increases your chances of long-term success. In my case, it has helped me pinpoint the times when I have lost my way and identify what happened during that period. Was there a particular project that kept me from working out and necessitated my eating takeout? Was there a period when travel accelerated? In short, just like with many other types of numbers discussed in this book, keeping track of them has no downside and only upside. Think of it as a game with yourself. As German fashion designer and artist Karl Lagerfeld was quoted as saying, "Dieting is the only game where you win when you lose!"

An alternative to weighing yourself is picking one piece or a few pieces of clothing and noticing how loose they can feel when you are experiencing your better days or weeks. Take a mental note of which clothes fit looser and using them as a benchmark. I have shirts that fit only when I am at my lightest or thinnest. When I want to know how I am doing, I try them on. Being able to wear them comfortably is a great feeling and an indicator that I am at my best.

EXERCISE

It is exercise alone that supports the spirits and keeps the mind in vigor.
—MARCUS TULLIUS CICERO

Exercise is the classic no-brainer. Like every other living thing on the planet, *Homo sapiens* need to be in motion. We did not evolve to be hunched in front of a screen or slouched on a couch. Bodies physiologically atrophy without activity—muscles become weak, blood circulation poor, joints rigid. Think about exercise in the abstract: Isn't it the very definition of *common sense?*

Here, I need to pause. My exercise recommendations are not for everyone. If you're differently abled, injured, or in chronic pain, any physical activity might be a heroic effort. We should never underestimate the massive achievement physical movement is for people living with pain or who are differently abled. Anything that engages the body, improves circulation, and flexes the joints can be a more significant effort than a daily 5K for others. Therefore, my suggestions are for those without such physical challenges; for those of you who have them, follow the therapies your medical professionals and caregivers recommend, and give yourself credit for the effort.

WILLFUL NEGLECT

In hardly any other arena of human behavior is there such a disconnect between intellectually comprehending the need for exercise and acting on that understanding. Especially in convenient luxury societies like the US, most people just don't get it.

According to the National Center for Health Statistics, in 2017, only a quarter of American adults met the recommended physical-activity, aerobic-activity, and muscle-strengthening guidelines.[78] These guidelines are far from stringent suggestions: at least two and a half hours of moderate-intensity or one hour and fifteen minutes

---

[78] https://www.cdc.gov/nchs/data/hus/2018/025.pdf.

of vigorous-intensity aerobic physical exercise per week. Less than 5 percent of adults participate in thirty minutes of physical activity each day.

People stubbornly resist not only the edict of evolution but the universal admonishments of doctors and scientists. I believe this shocking resistance to such a self-evident benefit represents me-of-today thinking on steroids. It's willful blindness to the inevitable results of this neglect, consigning the me of tomorrow to incapacity and needless suffering.

THE FIFTY-EIGHTY CURVE

Earlier in the chapter, I referenced the shape of what I call the fifty-eighty curve. Keeping the curve as flat as possible will afford the me of tomorrow the health and vitality to enjoy that wealth and leisure we dream of for our golden years—the reward for all those years of striving. It will also suppress sickness and help harden that vital immune system we need in these days of viruses.

One of my inspirations for focusing on this curve comes from the 2004 book *Younger Next Year* by Chris Crowley and his doctor, the late Henry Lodge.[79] The book was written for men, although its principles apply to women too. Crowley's work shows how people can become functionally younger every year even after age fifty, enabling them to live like fifty-year-olds until well into their eighties. While I was an amateur runner, I met living, breathing examples of these people. If you've participated in large public races, you've probably experienced the same initial embarrassment as I have: being passed easily by much older participants. I became awestruck at the incredible performances of so many older people.

The real champions among them defy belief. In 2018, American Gene Dykes ran a full marathon in under three hours at age seventy.[80]

---

[79] Chris Crowley and Henry S. Lodge, *Younger Next Year: A Guide to Living like 50 Until You're 80 and Beyond* (New York: Workman Publishing, 2004).
[80] https://www.arrs.run/SA_Mara.htm.

In 2016, Canadian runner Ed Whitlock broke four hours in a race in Toronto.[81] Astonishingly, he was eighty-five years young. These are extraordinary humans. However, countless ordinary people show extraordinary physical capabilities well into old age. Healthline Media, a US-based provider of health and wellness information, has a nifty calculator that lets you estimate an average marathon time and pace for runners of your age and gender.[82] It's based on recorded times for twenty-one thousand US marathon runners. These averages are impressive—remember these are not elite runners, just regular folks like you and me. The average for twenty- to twenty-four-year-old men is 4:01:55 and women 4:28:59, so if you run a marathon in under four and a half hours, you are pretty average. However, the average for men over sixty-five—which includes runners in their eighties and nineties—is not that much longer: for men 5:06:59, for women 5:20:57. When you recognize that these runners are three to four times older than their twenty-year-old counterparts, only an hour slower seems incredible. That suggests a fifty-eighty curve with a very flat slope.

ACTIONS FOR THE BODY OF TOMORROW

Flattening the fifty-eighty curve is critical for the me of tomorrow. When the curve is left to its own devices, absent exercise, the evidence is clear: it will slope down sharply. There are so many reasons to care about your body of tomorrow, and one of them is sheer physical survival. When you reach your eighties—many tomorrows from now—there are simple physical actions for day-to-day survival, keys to health, and well-being. These include simple activities such as the following:

- getting up from a chair and sitting back down unaided

---

[81] https://www.podiumrunner.com/training/marathon-training/gene-dykes-my-best-race-and-how-i-achieved-it/.

[82] http://www.pace-calculator.com/marathon-pace-comparison.php.

- going up and down stairs
- lifting your body from the floor after a tumble
- pushing a heavy object away from you
- running or walking a mile in an emergency

In our twenties, thirties, and forties, these activities are simple. We don't give them a second thought. But in their later years, many people struggle with actions like these. A me-of-tomorrow thinker plans for the health of tomorrow, even if that tomorrow may be fifty or sixty years away. The only way to ensure that activities like these stay simple is to increase your strength through regular exercise today. It's never too late to start; it's building the habit into our daily lives that many of us find so challenging.

BUILDING THE EXERCISE HABIT

My exercise regimen is modest. Other than when I was training for marathons or half-marathons, I've always been too busy with parts of my string other than self (see chapter 2) to become really dedicated to physical fitness. However, for some people, fitness is part of their identities. I'll talk more about that in chapter 8.

However, we should all integrate a simple regular exercise program into our daily routine. And make this a habit. As James Clear brilliantly illuminates in his *Atomic Habits*, establishing life changes is more about systems than goals.[83] For exercise, how you change your process depends on where you're starting from. Exercise has three distinct components. All are equally important and necessary to build a healthy me of tomorrow.

---

[83] James Clear, *Atomic Habits: Tiny Changes, Remarkable Results—an Easy and Proven Way to Build Good Habits and Break Bad Ones* (New York: Avery, 2018).

1. AEROBIC ACTIVITY

This component builds heart and circulatory health. Statistics consistently show that aerobic activity correlates with lower risks of coronary heart disease, stroke, hypertension, type 2 diabetes, many cancers, anxiety, depression, Alzheimer's disease, and other dementias. Physically active adults also sleep better, have improved cognition, and have a better quality of life.

If you're starting from square one, you could do worse than follow the "Physical Activity Guidelines for Americans" from the US Department of Health and Human Services (HHS).[84] Shocking though this sounds, if you just meet these guidelines, you will be exercising more than 75 percent of the American public! These are modest steps appropriate to your life stage—in my view, not overly ambitious. The guidelines for active adults recommend between two and a half and five hours of moderate-intensity aerobic exercise or one hour and fifteen minutes to two and a half hours of vigorous-intensity aerobic activity per week.

The guidelines suggest that you don't need to exercise every day. However, according to James Clear's philosophy of habits, if you don't break down major life changes into microsteps, there's much less chance of successfully implementing them. I find it easier to make microchanges daily, such that exercise becomes a way of life and you miss it when you don't do it. The goal is consistency, not quantity. Suppose you prefer high-intensity activities like running, lap swimming, and biking. In that case, this can be as little as fifteen minutes a day. For moderate-intensity activities like brisk walking, gentle cycling, and doubles tennis, thirty minutes a day surpasses the minimum target.

---

[84] https://health.gov/sites/default/files/2019-09/Physical_Activity_Guidelines_2nd_edition.pdf.

2. STRENGTH TRAINING

The second component of our exercise habit aims to strengthen muscles and bones. These activities, although in themselves not aerobic, have the additional benefit of burning extra calories. But their most important benefit is that they dramatically increase our chances of performing those tasks at eighty that we do without thinking at fifty. It's a massive curve-flattening step. Traditional strength training often involved lifting relatively heavy objects to strengthen various muscle groups. All of the body's major muscle groups needed to be worked—legs, hips, back, abdomen, chest, shoulders, and arms. The mantra was "Don't overstress your muscles, but work them to the point where it would be hard to do another repetition of the exercise." Improvements in muscle strength and endurance are progressive over time. Increasing the amount of weight or the number of days a week will result in stronger muscles.

Although HHS guidelines recommend performing a range of these exercises on two or more days per week, I couldn't stick with it. Even though this represents a much lower time commitment than aerobic conditioning, the bad news is that this infrequency makes the habit harder to embed. Strength training is likely something you need to schedule and remember to save time for.

I found a different approach that worked almost as well that I adopted for many years: fifteen minutes every day, maybe just two to three reps of four to five key exercises. My friend Essdras, who trains people for a living, introduced me to it. This method is all about using your own body as weight. It uses a combination of push-ups, sit-ups, and lunges. Essdras advises varying them so you can use different groups of large muscles. Again, the goal is to make this a habit, as regular as a shower or checking the daily news. Like my friend Essdras's, many of these exercise routines are available on YouTube, tailored to different age groups and levels.

The most crucial element in creating a lasting exercise program is consistency. However modest your initial goal, just doing it every day is essential. If you don't follow through, it will fail. Start with a minimum threshold—something easily achievable. When I started, my goal was to walk thirty minutes a day—one lap of my neighborhood. That became a daily habit, and it felt unusual or strange if there was a day when I missed it. It's so much easier to build on an existing pattern.

For both new exercise habits—aerobic conditioning and strength training—the usual rules apply. Understand your body—its limitations, quirks, and nuances—and prepare it gradually for exertion. Stretching and bending will not only maximize the effect of exercise but help build flexibility and balance. Your me of many tomorrows from now will thank you!

3. STRETCHING

I believe stretching is the one area of physical fitness that gets overlooked. We all need greater flexibility. I remember Dr. Burns, my college health-and-fitness professor, pointing out to the class all those people religiously running around campus, telling us that, in all probability, few of them could touch their toes because they lacked flexibility. He equated good physical health with the need to be flexible.

This is an easy exercise to forget or dismiss. I neglected it for a long time and still fail every once in a while. The issue here is that it appears so simple and unimportant. The reality is that our leading sedentary lives or practicing the same sport over and over again only works specific muscles in certain ways. It doesn't provide the whole body with that other important element of fitness: flexibility.

CONCLUSION

My four components to ensuring a me of tomorrow may seem simple. However, they require a combination of understanding, planning, dedication, and balance. Committing to giving yourself the best-possible chance of achieving a healthy tomorrow, especially in this new era of deadly viruses, requires a high degree of mental discipline.

We must acknowledge that planning for the health of tomorrow is difficult. Poor food choices are all around us, there is insufficient time for exercise and sleep, and the commitment required to create stress management is not trivial. However, I can assure you that the rewards are worth the effort. Your Me @ Self deserves it.

Flattening the fifty-eighty curve will immeasurably enhance the quality of your long-term me of tomorrow. Besides, every tomorrow before then will also benefit. I used to think that getting older was something over which we had little or no control. As I have learned over time, there is a lot we can control about how the me of tomorrow ages. The me of tomorrow can age taking medicines and dealing with physical limitations. Or the me of tomorrow can age gracefully and more independently. The me of tomorrow who ages gracefully spends less money on medicine, avoids unnecessary trips to the doctor, doesn't need surgery for self-induced problems, and has more confidence because he or she is taking care of him- or herself.

Here's to futureproofing your immune system; enjoying many tomorrows; and building lifelong eating, exercise, sleep, and stress-management habits to make a stronger, healthier me of tomorrow.

CHAPTER 8

BUILDING YOUR STRATEGY

Don't stop thinking about tomorrow. Don't stop, it'll soon be here.
—FLEETWOOD MAC

We have come to the beginning of the end of this book. I hope you've found the ideas in it helpful and thought-provoking and the exercises useful. You may have heard some of these ideas before in different forms; however, I believe many of them have been shortchanged or neglected.

At heart, the principles I propose are fundamental. We need to look at situations, especially when confronted by critical decisions and also in our day-to-day lives, with a different set of lenses. Instead of a narrow, shortsighted lens that examines the here and now, we need to broaden our aperture. These new lenses require us to focus both on today and tomorrow.

The manual has provided advice in six areas:

1. A balanced life
2. Lifetime learning
3. Relationships

4. Careers
5. Wealth
6. Health

I have proposed practical planning exercises in most of these areas to help you apply me-of-tomorrow thinking. The approaches outlined have worked for me for many years and also for many people I know. The frameworks include the following:

- a new approach about the way to balance your life using the metaphor of a finite length of string—the sum total of your time and energy
- compelling reasons to become a truth seeker and how to harness the power of continual learning
- exercises to begin that truth-seeking journey if you're relatively new to it
- tools to build your network (is it really just professional?)
- a method to practice a relationship tune-up
- a different way to approach career progression and to understand some of the values that will bring you career success
- a new measure of wealth and sound advice to improve your financial situation
- how to diffuse those nagging "truths" that cause stress

ME-OF-TOMORROW TACTICS

Think of these exercises as me-of-tomorrow tactics. They will help you improve many areas of life. They should be informative and actionable.

However, putting on this new set of lenses and changing existing decision-making habits are not easy. They run contrary to many of our common instincts and conflict with many messages that bombard us daily.

However, life is busy, and time is short. Combing through these layers of advice and exercises might seem daunting. So if you think anything like me, you will have three questions:

1. Where do I start?
2. What do I do with these ideas?
3. What have I learned that I could apply?

Hopefully, you want to try on some of these new ideas. Perhaps there's a particular exercise that seems to address what you're wrestling with right now. This final chapter is about building a strategy to prioritize and structure your planning. It will help you accelerate along the road to a me-of-tomorrow mindset. You will be able to build your unique strategy to become a better planner for life's journey. It all begins with some serious stocktaking.

TAKING STOCK

Before you can build an effective strategy to apply the learnings in this book, it's essential that you understand where you are. You have to start from where you are; there's no other place from where to start! All of us approach this thinking from different starting places. Some people already envisage and plan for their futures when they make decisions, but not in my structured, businesslike way. For others, the idea of taking your many future mes into account is a novel concept.

If you are already a me-of-tomorrow thinker, hopefully the ideas and exercises in this book will help you fine-tune and refocus your efforts. If you have a more instinctive, by-the-seat-of-your-pants approach to planning, then now may be the time to strategize how to integrate some of the ideas and exercises into your daily life.

Remember—it's never too late to integrate disciplined future planning into your life. Even if you are long into your career and relationships, a new approach will help you maximize all those future tomorrows that are still ahead. Any time is a good one to take stock.

RECOGNIZING OUR DECISION PATTERNS

An unscientific survey of my acquaintances and mentees suggests me-of-tomorrow thinking remains the exception rather than the rule. Even with these exceptions, this approach is often limited to one of life's domains, usually Me @ Work. I've noticed that the ideas are missing most among early career professionals—ironically, the people who would benefit the most.

By contrast, many people have developed decision-making habits that inhibit future happiness. Most of the time, they don't even realize it. Decision-making methods and the decisions that flow from them grow into patterns of thought and behavior. Often, many people aren't sufficiently observant or self-aware to recognize these patterns—patterns that tell us a great deal about where we are.

Habits are hard both to create and to break. As they accumulate, habits become part of our personas. If you observe carefully, you can catch yourself repeating the same mistakes. Often, these are mistakes you're not even aware of. Maybe it's spending another hour in the office when you promised to be home for dinner. Or not returning your sister's call. Or turning on the TV instead of listening to an audiobook. Eating an extra slice of pizza. Buying an expensive purse you don't need. These decisions become unconscious. We make them like automatons. They have become those habits that are so hard to break.

COURSE CORRECTIONS

Whatever your situation, I believe it's never too late to change your planning and decision-making patterns and hence your behaviors. In this chapter, I urge you to reflect on these decision-making patterns and understand how they've become embedded in your persona. We all need to reflect on these habits and recognize whether they're conscious choices or the result of unbroken patterns. And ask the crucial question, Are they helping the me of tomorrow?

Most of us know the saying, attributed to author Gretchen Rubin and often quoted in the context of raising children, "The days are long, but the years are short."[85] It's a universal truth: before we know it, many tomorrows will have flowed past. Like setting a slightly misdirected course on a long voyage, a few degrees' marginal error will take us to the completely wrong destination. Many times, I woke up and realized that my course was off and needed correcting. Sometimes it's just a tweak of the rudder; at other times, it's much more radical. At one point, I was investing too much time and energy in chasing a promotion and new title at work. I was neglecting vital relationships in pursuit of my career ambitions. Often, I couldn't free myself to focus on my real aspirations, such as writing books, coaching and mentoring young people, and ensuring my wife and children were seeing the best of me. Understanding the long-term consequences of such me-of-today thinking caused me to take stock and reprioritize my life.

One way of identifying errors in our course and speed is to do some stocktaking. Hit the Pause button and review. Over time, I realized the importance of remapping my plans for tomorrow, of taking stock of those habits and patterns that were creeping into my life. Sitting down and looking at my life through a proper me-of-tomorrow lens and going through planning exercises across all of life's domains.

Without fail, that conscious act of refocusing—doing the exercises laid out in this book—always made me change my behaviors. My life became my teacher, provided I took the time to stop and realize how today's actions impacted all the many mes of many tomorrows

---

[85] Gretchen Rubin, *The Happiness Project: Or Why I Spent a Year Trying to Sing in the Morning, Clean My Closets, Fight Right, Read Aristotle, and Generally Have More Fun* (New York: Harper, 2009).

to come. However, one other reason behavior is hard to change and patterns become entrenched is because of what I call *our armor*.

OUR ARMOR

I referred to this armor in chapter 1. By *armor*, I refer to that peculiar bundle of ideas, personality quirks, hang-ups, and illusions that we all wear. Every morning, this armor is the image we present to the world. The armor is not only a picture of how we like others to see us; it's also, more often than not, how we see ourselves. It's the source of our self-confidence, the persona that will get us through the day ahead.

Our armor doesn't imply we are just actors playing roles. We can think of our armor as our personal brands or the masks we wear. Actually, it's more deep-seated than that. Besides public figures, few people can pull off a complete branding exercise every day of their lives. Even the most controlled people can't fake authenticity for long. Furthermore, trying too hard to create an inauthentic persona rarely survives contact with the rigors of daily life. The armor isn't just what we want to portray but also reflects, to a great degree, who we are and what we value.

Often, our choice of armor gets in the way of creating a fulfilling future. In this book's language, today's armor becomes a barrier to fulfilling mes of tomorrow. Maybe we are unable to maintain the prime fitness and smartness that were our hallmark and we deprive ourselves of family and relationships to maintain an image of prosperity. Or we may squander our wealth of tomorrow by dressing for success, denying ourselves precious me time, or failing to realize our personal dreams.

Another metaphor for this armor is the act of standing in front of a set of mirrored dresser drawers. Every morning we look in that mirror. Since we were young, we have learned to reach into that top drawer and pull out something that gives us the belief we hold on to to face the day. That thing we pull out provides us with the confidence to be who we are. Some of us pull out our hard-worker skills; others pull out good looks; and some pull out athletic ability. Reaching in and plucking out that item becomes the persona we show the world. As T. S. Eliot wrote, "There will be time / To prepare a face to meet the faces that you meet."[86] We want people to see us in a particular way, and often it's how we come to see ourselves too.

Our armor or tool to face the day usually starts as a conscious choice. However, some of us stumble into our armor because of how we think other people perceive us. It's often easier to go with the flow than to create a new persona that flies in the face of evidence. To illustrate what I'm talking about, here are some typical examples of the armor people choose.

ARMOR EXAMPLES

Here are some classic examples of personal armor I've observed throughout my life and career. Some of these are a little exaggerated, but you get the idea!

1. THE SMARTEST PERSON IN THE ROOM

If you were born or developed a fast mental processor, a quick turn of phrase, or had the education to be exposed to complex ideas and absorbed them, think yourself lucky. There are many such people in many walks of life. The armor these people often display is intellectual mastery, superior knowledge, and hidden wisdom. They get their fuel for life from an effortless grasp of facts and arguments. Perhaps it makes them feel superior, in command, several steps ahead of the average Joe or Jill.

In reality, the decision-making habits of these smart people are likely far from perfect. In the language of chapter 3, they are more

---

[86] T. S. Eliot, "The Love Song of J. Alfred Prufrock."

likely to be truth owners than truth seekers, unaware of their blind spots. They are less likely to be curious. Smart may feel satisfying, but filling those smart shoes over a lifetime can be too unrewarding. Life balance will favor Me @ Self and Me @ Work over other parts of the string.[87]

Furthermore, the smart-guy or smart-gal persona requires sounding good—not a recipe for developing healthy relationships. The smartest person in the room is typically not the most liked or the one other people gravitate toward. They don't make influential leaders. Sure, leaders may be smart, but they are usually not the smartest. The smart person is more likely an adviser, omitted from real decision-making, sometimes frustrated as others mangle their ideas and exclude them from planning and action.

2. DRESSED FOR SUCCESS

Armor for these people is based on looking good. It may be because of physical appearance, perhaps their well-toned abs and slim physique. Or it may be based on personal grooming—beautiful clothes, hair, and makeup. The message is that they are poised, professional, and in control. Their physical advantages make them able and willing to push themselves and exert more energy than others.

There is real psychology about dressing for success. Who among us doesn't feel that little bit more confident if we are wearing perfect clothes, for example? One 2014 study showed that well-dressed individuals are more successful negotiators.[88] Another study even suggested that well-dressed people are more likely to engage in big-picture thinking. According to Columbia professor Michael Slepian,

---

[87] Chapter 2 (The String Hypothesis).
[88] https://www.businessinsider.com/dressing-for-success-actually-works-2017-7?r=US&IR=T.

the study's coauthor, "When you feel more powerful, you don't have to focus on the details."[89]

However, it's worth questioning whether this persona can last a lifetime. What trade-offs does this persona demand? Does the necessary Me @ Self time hurt family or other relationships? How can we maintain this persona as we age and lose energy? What financial commitments do we make to continue to dress for success throughout a long career? One excuse I often hear from this persona is that "my job requires me to dress this way." While some professional roles do require a particularly polished look, there are ways to achieve this while still keeping an eye on building wealth. If you can't do this, then perhaps a change of career is the best choice. A profession where so much income is spent on presentation may not be worth pursuing.

3. THE BUDDING TYCOON

Most of us have known people who seem to ooze money and status. They may have beautiful houses, expensive cars, and exclusive golf or country club memberships, or they may take holidays in exotic locations. They're typically not shy about showing off their apparent wealth. This assumed affluence is the key to their self-confidence. It tells people that they have been successful, even though, in reality, the source of their spending might have nothing to do with success.

As I pointed out in chapter 6, shows of opulence tell us little about someone's wealth. A showy person may be genuinely wealthy, but he or she might just as easily be at level 1 or 2 on my wealth scale presented in that chapter, effectively living from hand to mouth. Showcasing luxury might just be that: a showcase that gives such people artificial confidence.

As with dressing for success, which is related, playing the budding tycoon requires us to maintain this persona over a period of time.

---

[89] Michael L. Slepian and others, "The Cognitive Consequences of Formal Clothing," *Social Psychological and Personality Science* 6, no. 6 (2015): 661–68, https://doi.org/10.1177/1948550615579462.

Even if we are showing spending and wealth, we need a level of income that, more often than not, will drive us to focus on work and career, thereby depriving our other life domains: self, community and friendship, and spirituality.

4. THE ENTHUSIASTIC CARER

Enthusiasm is one of life's greatest virtues, and caring is one of humanity's most beautiful attributes. Some people embrace these two attributes, and the world is often better for it. Many of us strive for it but realize we often fall short. Because of its inherent decency, it is a persona some people choose. Their fuel for life is the persona of caring about everyone and everything. They are always the first to jump in and help someone in trouble or to fix problems.

However, these kind folks tend to struggle with their string allocation. They often relegate their own needs to other people's. For example, their careers could suffer, as they have insufficient time to focus on them.

Related to this, the shadow of can-do enthusiasm is a commonly understood phenomenon. Always volunteering to solve problems and provide others with cheerleading and support can sap your energy and resources. Once established, this persona allows others to sit back and expect you to pick up the slack. That is, knowing that you will step up allows others to step back. And even the most enthusiastic carer is not immune from feelings of resentment: think of the countless examples of family friction caused by one child taking on an undue burden of caring for sick or elderly parents.

Maybe you can see yourself in one of these armor choices. Or at least a flash of recognition? These are examples of the types of armor or game face some people choose to present to the world. As these archetypes show, life can become dangerously unbalanced if we cruise along with established patterns and habits.

CHOOSING OUR ARMOR

Whether we recognize these archetypes or whether we find it challenging to identify what armor we put on every day, one point is clear: we can all choose to change our armor. And we should all anticipate the trade-offs and sacrifices our choices create.

This starts with appreciating how others see us. Awareness of our armor can help us decide if we want to continue grabbing those items from our metaphorical drawers every morning for the rest of our lives. Change requires honest reflection, an appreciation of where we draw our reservoir of confidence, and determination regarding the new armor we want to adopt.

EPHEMERAL VERSUS DURABLE ARMOR

One of the most important lessons about our armor is that life is more comfortable if we choose armor that lasts. It's much better to draw our self-worth from values that are permanent, not transitory. I remember thinking about this when my daughter was still in elementary school. Like many little girls her age, she was active in sports, played a musical instrument, and got good grades.

At night, we talked about why I loved her. I would ask her, "Does Daddy love you because of your grades at school? Does Daddy love you because you are a fast swimmer? Does Daddy love you because you are pretty? Does Daddy love you because you can play the violin?"

I had taught her that the answer to all of those was no! The right answer was "Daddy loves me for who I am."

Of course, I was trying to teach her to build self-esteem independent of her sporting, musical, and academic accomplishments, as well as her physical appearance, something many girls and young women feel pressure about. These accomplishments are ephemeral or incidental. Even if she stopped swimming, finished playing the violin, or struggled at school, she would never lose a feeling of paternal love. I wanted her to learn to derive her self-esteem from something that couldn't break or change with time.

There's a parallel in our adult world. So many armor choices are similarly fleeting. For example, we all see Hollywood actors who continue to submit to the plastic surgeon's knife because they want to look younger than they are. Their looks are essential to them. Their appearance is their armor. Other actors age without much concern because their faces do not define them. They derive their armor from something else.

Many people spend long hours at work without needing to. They are already well off and play critical roles in their organizations. However, they wear their titles and responsibilities as their armor, believing them to be as important as, or more important than, the money they make. Regardless, their jobs are the most critical aspects of who they are.

We see people who are always impeccably dressed, whether going to a party or the grocery store. Every morning, they pull out the well-dressed characteristic from their drawers—literally! That characteristic defines who they are. They carry around the appreciation and admiration of the world based on this.

Whatever armor we choose, because it matters to us, we believe others' love and appreciation for us is tied to it. We think that if we didn't wear that armor, people wouldn't appreciate us as much. Like my earlier examples, these ideas are fatal for life balance and me-of-tomorrow thinking.

This pervasive habit is the wrong way to pursue long-term happiness. For example, some people believe money will make them happier. They think they will be happier with better cars or bigger houses. Unfortunately, this doesn't work. A new car can be another confidence-boosting item to add to your morning repertoire if you tend to gravitate toward such big-ticket items. You buy the car—and the fancy-car confidence that comes with it—and let that define you. You may feel cooler, better, or more attractive because you have the latest model. But these ideas are just in your head. People care a heck of a lot less about them than you do. People may comment and recognize you have a nice car, but that thought disappears from their heads much faster than you think.

As we have discussed, where you derive your confidence from has a significant impact on how you will spend your time and what will happen as a result of that. For example, if being a health nut drives your self-confidence, you will probably live longer and be in better shape than those around you. Pick your job to define your identity, and you could end up with a less-than-ideal outcome when it comes to relationships or health.

Consequently, we must distinguish permanent sources of self-confidence from those that are transitory. Society puts tremendous pressure on us, affecting how we feel and how we think *others* think about us. Many of us continuously worry about other people's material possessions, jobs, marital statuses, and so forth. A better model for the me of tomorrow is to develop confidence from timeless things that we can control through our actions. If we don't do this, we may end up on a hamster wheel. To paraphrase a famous adage, we end up buying things we don't need to impress people we don't care for and who don't care for us.

BUILDING YOUR STRATEGIC PLAN

Understanding your armor is that stocktaking step that enables you to identify and understand its impact on your daily decision-making. Understanding and choosing to change your armor should be part of your strategic plan.

This self-examination has other benefits too. You will understand how you make decisions, why you make the decisions you do, and your decisions' effects on all aspects of your life.

Here are some typical questions you might ask yourself:

- What gives me confidence?
- What helps me make it through the day?
- Am I fueling my life the right way?

- What will my life look like if I continue fueling my confidence in the same way?
- If I lose my money, my looks, or my job, will my friends continue being my friends?
- Are my friends actually just friends of my house, my car, or my title, or are they my real friends?
- Will I be rich but without great kids?
- Will I be in great shape but alone?
- Will I have a great career but no friends?
- Am I making sacrifices that my me of tomorrow will chastise me for?
- Is it too late to make changes? (Hint: the answer is never!)

Now that you're thinking creatively with a me-of-tomorrow mindset, I suggest building a matrix like the one in figure 12. Realize that you're working against nature. It doesn't allow you to think more long-term. With that in mind, be purposeful. Write down your goals. Check them from time to time.

Another smart way to get things done is to share your goals with others. Chose those who are closest to you or most impacted by your actions and decisions. Are the goals related to how you balance your life, what you do at work, how much money you save, or how many hours you will sleep? Write them down and share them.

I have put a few ideas into some of the cells of figure 12 to get you started. However, make this matrix your own. Be honest about where you are in each dimension, and think aspirationally and realistically about where you want to be. The implications of failing to embrace me-of-tomorrow thinking should by now be clear.

Aspect	Where I Am	Where I Want to Be	The Implications of Not Changing
		(Choose multiple timelines—for example, one year and five years.)	

Life balance	Balanced? Unbalanced? Which aspect of me is about right, and which one is not?	What area needs balancing?	What will suffer if I don't change (e.g., health or relationships)?
Continuous learning	What's my score, from 1 to 10? Am I a learner or a truth owner?	Choose an area of learning. It can be a technical area or leadership. It can also be learning about relationships.	What will suffer if I don't improve my score? Can I learn to take better care of myself? Can I learn to understand others better?
Relationships	Who needs more of my time? Who needs less of my time?	Where do I want to be in terms of friends, family, and professional relationships?	Who would visit me in the hospital if I ever got sick? Who would be truly worried for me?
Career	What is my position or title? What is my level of influence? Do I exhibit the right behaviors?	What do I want my job to mean to me in a few years?	What happens if I work too much? Who and what suffer?
Wealth	What level of wealth do I have today?	What will my wealth level be in a year?	How much stress will I have if I don't change my habits? How free will I feel if I start thinking differently about saving?
Health	What are my food patterns? What are my exercise habits? How am I sleeping? How much stress do I feel?	Pick at least one area to improve in.	Which first-world diseases are more likely to impact me because of my current behavior?

Figure 12.

This is a lot to absorb and process. If you have done this thoughtfully, you might have a complicated matrix. This process may have taken you several days or even weeks to complete.

You now have the structure of a strategic plan. You have your SWOT (strengths, weaknesses, opportunities, threats) analysis. But another key question remains: What should you work on first?

SO WHERE DO I START?

Think of the different elements of your life as links in a chain. The links are your life balance, continuous learning, relationships, career, wealth, and health. The chain makes up your complete life—the total you. Each area is important; for example, it's useless being wealthy if you don't have the health to enjoy it or having a successful career if it makes your relationships suffer.

Once you have a strategic action plan, think about each element in the chain. To paraphrase that two-hundred-year-old saying, "You're only as strong as your weakest link."[90] What is your weakest link? What is the most immediate need? You can't half solve each of your links. You need to bring your me of tomorrow to each of them.

During the strategic-planning exercise, evaluate each link as it

---

[90] https://books.google.co.uk/books/about/Essays_on_the_Intellectual_Powers_of_Man.html?id=3AcQAAAAYAAJ&printsec=frontcover&source=kp_read_button&redir_esc=y#v=onepage&q=chain&f=false.

currently stands and determine where you want to be. Perhaps you are close to perfect in one or more areas and need just a tweak, or maybe you feel out of balance, as though you're behind on learning, suffering in your career and relationships, and worried about health and money.

Your evaluation of each link will vary depending on your expectations of success and the level of self-confidence you have in each area. But you should be able to identify your weakest link. If you know it's your spousal relationship, focus on that first. If you are drastically overweight and stressed, there is nothing better to start with than a diet-and-exercise program that integrates sleep and stress management. You will find that tackling one link will bring about success and open up opportunities to work on other parts of the chain.

Another metaphor I like to use for my plan is a bridge. I want a future, and to achieve it, I need to build the bridge to that future. What do I focus on first? It's a slightly more positive approach than thinking about a weak link, and it should be more about building something rather than bridging a gap. Regardless of how you approach it, the outcome should be the same: a plan based on what matters most to you.

Remember the goal. In every significant area of life—balance, learning, relationships, career, wealth, and health—every decision we make, every move we make, has profound implications for our future well-being. It is that future well-being—that me of tomorrow—that will make all this effort worthwhile. Soon this planning will get easier and become second nature.

CONCLUSION

So you might be wondering what my armor or persona is. After much trial and error and many adjustments along the way, I found that the only armor I needed was that trusty old swiss army knife! All of life's domains are equally important; none matters more than any of the others. What I strive for continually—not always with success—is balance. Disciplined thinking about my learning, relationships, career, wealth, and health using me-of-tomorrow lenses has taught me how to develop better habits, more balanced approaches, and plans that I could adopt with minimum fuss and stress.

Now my strategic plans are periodic revisions of the old. With goals set, I can measure my progress and continuously reappraise for one year, two years, five years, and even ten years from now. It's great to look back and see how you performed against the goals that you set. Now you're in the tomorrow—is that original mental picture anything like your current reality? How can you plan better now that you have the experience of having lived the plan?

The freedom of having ongoing plans is that you can make your major decisions within a context and a structure. You don't have to continually question assumptions and processes. The me of tomorrow has that critical seat at the decision-making table. Decisions are easier to make. This keeps your eyes on the prize: a better me of tomorrow.

EPILOGUE

Every day, we are bombarded with advice on how to live better lives. Suggestions for better health, greater wealth, and perfect happiness are everywhere. This torrent of information and disinformation, rampant on social media, makes it challenging for us to arrange our priorities and even harder to produce an effective plan. Life in the 2020s is so uncertain and replete with contradictory advice based on sketchy data. Thank you for reading about my ideas. I like to think they are practical and straightforward. The opinions and recommendations are my own, and where they rely on data, I have tried to show the source.

This book sets out my life philosophy and includes what I consider fundamental truths about life. I am explicit in my emphasis on life balance, lifetime learning, personal relationships, career development, wealth, and health. These ideas draw on my own experience, as well as the wisdom of many other thinkers and writers, ancient and modern, most of whom I have tried to acknowledge. Some of these ideas took me years to form and develop. One of my goals in writing them down is to help you learn faster than I did. You will save time, and you can use that time for other aspects of your life. Please think of this as a life-planning manual that takes many ideas and filters from my hard-won wisdom.

However, my overriding message is not in these individual suggestions. You may have your own working philosophies on health, saving, reading, and relationships, for example. Mine have served me well. By all means, follow your own tips and tricks to get fit, stash away your freedom fund, and become an eternal truth seeker.

My key message is that all the advice in the world doesn't matter if you don't commit to the process of planning. This commitment means that you need to integrate me-of-tomorrow thinking into all elements of your life. Suspend the urgings of instant gratification, and plan for all those many future selves—your own mes of tomorrow. Doing this seriously and systematically will dramatically improve your future.

Envisage those future mes. Get to know them. And always plan your actions with those people in mind. That doesn't mean sacrificing today for tomorrow. It means giving tomorrow a seat at the decision-making table. In the scramble and chaos of life, there's no point in throwing up your hands and doubting that there will be a tomorrow. For most of us, happily, there will be—*many* tomorrows, in fact. So enjoy the planning—it's a huge step up from dreaming, and it will help you avoid some pain and enhance your happiness in your future tomorrows. Here's to the me of tomorrow!

BIBLIOGRAPHY

Benson, Herbert, and Miriam Z. Klipper. *The Relaxation Response.* Updated and expanded ed. New York: Quill, 2001.

Campbell, T. Colin, and Thomas M. Campbell. *The China Study: The Most Comprehensive Study of Nutrition Ever Conducted and the Startling Implications for Diet, Weight Loss and Long-Term Health.* 1st BenBella Books ed. Dallas: BenBella Books, 2005.

Chattu, Vijay Kumar, Dilshad Manzar, Soosanna Kumary, Deepa Burman, David Warren Spence, and Seithikurippu R. Pandi-Perumal. "The Global Problem of Insufficient Sleep and Its Serious Public Health Implications." *Healthcare* 7, no. 1 (2018): 1. https://doi.org/10.3390/healthcare7010001.

Clear, James. *Atomic Habits: Tiny Changes, Remarkable Results—an Easy and Proven Way to Build Good Habits and Break Bad Ones.* New York: Avery, 2018.

Collins, James C. *Good to Great: Why Some Companies Make the Leap—and Others Don't.* New York: HarperBusiness, 2001.

Corley, Thomas, C. *Rich Habits: The Daily Success Habits of Wealthy Individuals.* Minneapolis: Langdon Street Press, 2009.

Covey, Stephen R. *The 7 Habits of Highly Effective People: Powerful Lessons in Personal Change.* 25th anniversary ed. New York: Simon & Schuster, 2013.

Crowley, Chris, and Henry S. Lodge. *Younger Next Year: A Guide to Living like 50 Until You're 80 and Beyond.* New York: Workman Publishing, 2004.

Daly, John A. *Advocacy: Championing Ideas and Influencing Others.* New Haven: Yale University Press, 2011.

Duhigg, Charles. *The Power of Habit: Why We Do What We Do in Life and Business.* New York: Random House Trade Paperbacks, 2014.

Eggerichs, Emerson. *Love and Respect: The Love She Most Desires, the Respect He Desperately Needs.* Nashville: Integrity Publishers, 2004.

Granovetter, Mark S. "The Strength of Weak Ties." *American Journal of Sociology* 78, no. 6 (1973): 1360–80. https://doi.org/10.1086/225469.

Haidt, Jonathan. *The Happiness Hypothesis: Finding Modern Truth in Ancient Wisdom.* New York: Basic Books, 2006.

Kahneman, Daniel. *Thinking, Fast and Slow.* New York: Farrar, Straus and Giroux, 2013.

Lappé, Frances Moore, and Marika Hahn. *Diet for a Small Planet.* New York: Ballantine Books, 2010.

Leger, Kate A., Susan T. Charles, and David M. Almeida. "Let It Go: Lingering Negative Affect in Response to Daily Stressors Is Associated with Physical Health Years Later."

Psychological Science 29, no. 8 (2018): 1283–90. https://doi.org/10.1177/0956797618763097.

Lockett, Katherine, and Jeni Mumford. *Work/Life Balance for Dummies*. Chichester, UK: John Wiley, 2009.

Manson, Mark. *The Subtle Art of Not Giving a F*ck: A Counterintuitive Approach to Living a Good Life*. New York: HarperOne, 2016.

Mautz, Scott. *Find the Fire: Ignite Your Inspiration—and Make Work Exciting Again*. New York: AMACOM, American Management Association, 2017.

Moss, Michael. *Salt, Sugar, Fat: How the Food Giants Hooked Us*. Toronto: Signal, 2013.

Pollan, Michael. *In Defense of Food: An Eater's Manifesto*. New York: Penguin Press, 2008.

Pollan, Michael. *The Omnivore's Dilemma: A Natural History of Four Meals*. New York: Penguin Press, 2006.

Qin, Pengmin, and Georg Northoff. "How Is Our Self Related to Midline Regions and the Default-Mode Network?" *NeuroImage* 57, no. 3 (2011): 1221–33.

Rubin, Gretchen. *The Happiness Project: Or Why I Spent a Year Trying to Sing in the Morning, Clean My Closets, Fight Right, Read Aristotle, and Generally Have More Fun*. New York: Harper, 2009.

Slepian, Michael L., Simon N. Ferber, Joshua M. Gold, and Abraham M. Rutchick. "The Cognitive Consequences of Formal Clothing." *Social Psychological and Personality Science* 6, no. 6 (2015): 661–68. https://doi.org/10.1177/1948550615579462.

Stanley, Thomas J., and William D. Danko. *The Millionaire Next Door: The Surprising Secrets of America's Wealthy*. 25th anniversary ed. Lanham: Taylor Trade Publishing, 2016.

Thaler, Richard H. *Misbehaving: The Making of Behavioral Economics*. New York: W.W. Norton, 2015.

Walker, Matthew. *Why We Sleep: The New Science of Sleep and Dreams*. London: Penguin Books, 2018.

Watson, Nathaniel F., Ilene M. Rosen, Ronald D. Chervin, and Board of Directors of the American Academy of Sleep Medicine. "The Past Is Prologue: The Future of Sleep Medicine." *Journal of Clinical Sleep Medicine* 13, no. 1 (2017): 127–35. https://doi.org/10.5664/jcsm.6406.

Willett, W. C. "Balancing Life-Style and Genomics Research for Disease Prevention." *Science* 296, no. 5568 (2002): 695–98. https://doi.org/10.1126/science.1071055.

Williams, Joan C., and Heather Boushey. *The Three Faces of Work-Family Conflict: The Poor, the Professionals, and the Missing*. 2010.

ACKNOWLEDGMENTS

This book has been more than twenty years in the making. People too numerous to mention have provided the examples and inspiration for many of the ideas it contains. They are all part of this book, and I thank them for being part of my life.

Yogesh was the first person who heard my thoughts about how to plan for a better life and told me I should write a book. Later, I heard the same mantra multiple times from several other people who'd listened to my ideas about more balanced living. Ultimately, however, the impetus for eventually writing it all came down to two driving forces: (1) my dad, who always encouraged me to write a book, and (2) a conversation I had with Juan Carlos on a lazy afternoon in 2019. I told him about my plans to write a book. He told me to stop thinking about it and just do it. His push was the straw that broke the camel's back in persuading me to move forward.

As Nick and I worked through the manuscript, several wonderful people offered help selflessly, took their time to review, and provided invaluable advice: Shabnam; Dario; Jhovanny; Payal; Pete; my supportive wife, Mariela; Nick's wife, Jerrie; and Ximena, who provided invaluable ideas and help with the cover. I thank them all for their ideas, time, and encouragement.

Lastly, I am incredibly grateful to Nick for helping me bring this work across the finish line. He is a great friend but also someone who challenges me intellectually.

ABOUT THE AUTHOR

Efrain Rovira is an individual with an insatiable intellectual curiosity. A native of Panama, he came to the US on a Walton Foundation Scholarship. After moving between Panama and the US a few times, he planted roots in Texas. Although he has spent most of his career in high tech and by traditional measures has been very successful, he is most proud of what he has accomplished as a father, husband, son, brother, and friend.

In business, he has led sales, marketing, strategy, channel, product management, and marketing communications at the executive level in Fortune 10 companies. He has also been the general manager of multibillion-dollar businesses globally and regionally.

Efrain enjoys developing plans about how to grow. For him, growth is about not just business growth but also personal growth. He has coached and mentored many successful executives and budding entrepreneurs. He offers advice beyond standard professional development and executive mentorship, helping people think about their careers in the broader context of their whole lives and their plans. Efrain loves to build mental models of all aspects of life – developing formulas for living better. He has captured many of these coaching ideas and models in *The Me of Tomorrow,* his first book.

Efrain's ghostwriter, Nick Collins, helped put these ideas down on paper. Efrain and Nick have been friends and business associates for more than twenty years. Nick has pressure-tested many of Efrain's ideas and challenged them with his blend of curiosity and skepticism, choosing to adopt many of them as life challenges along the way. Nick is an Anglo-American market strategist and researcher currently living near Oxford in England.

CPSIA information can be obtained
at www.ICGtesting.com
Printed in the USA
LVHW101410290422
717569LV00011B/108/J

9 781663 229069